The Girl's Guide

to

Social

Savvy

Manners for the Modern World

Jodi R. R. Smith

BARNES & NOBLE BOOKS

NEW YORK

For my Mother and Grandmother, who know that every mother is a working mother and who taught me to do if you think you can, even when others tell you that you can't.

Acknowledgments

This book could not have come to be without the support and help of many people, including: Hallie Einhorn, who found me; Ginger Burr, who saw in me a spark I did not yet see in myself; Judith Halpern, for her eagle eye; Roberta Winter, who knows it takes a village; Paulette Agne, for helping me trust the universe; Lisa, Kim, Jen, Amy, Sabrina, Robin, Ellen, and my other friends who insisted I could even when I thought I could not. I would also like to thank the thousands of people who have participated in my seminars and written to me via the web.

A BARNES & NOBLE BOOK

Text ©2004 by Jodi R. R. Smith
Illustrations ©2004 by Bill Reid

Library of Congress Cataloging-in-Publication Data

Smith, Jodi R. R.
  The girl's guide to social savvy : manners for the modern world / Jodi R.R. Smith.
    p. cm.
  ISBN 0-7607-4938-8 (alk. paper)
  1. Etiquette for women. I. Title.

  BJ1856.S62 2004
  395.1'44--dc22

                                              2003023467

Printed and bound in China by Midas Printing

1 3 5 7 9 10 8 6 4 2

contents

Have you ever noticed that there are some people to whom you take an instant liking? You enjoy speaking with them and look forward to seeing them again. Conversely, there are those who make you feel uncomfortable whenever you're around them. While you may not be able to put your finger on the exact reason, as soon as you start talking to such a person, you wish that you were somewhere else. Often, these reactions are caused by the other individual's mastery of social savvy.

Social savvy is about knowing how to behave in different situations. The socially savvy woman is comfortable in a variety of environments and is able to make those around her comfortable as well. While it may seem as though she has some inherent capability for knowing exactly how to behave in different situations and how to interact with different individuals, this is not the case. In fact, the big secret is that people are not born socially savvy, but that the trait is actually a learned skill. And it is not a difficult one. While etiquette may seem like a daunting subject, it's really quite simple, centering upon respect, consideration for others, and common sense. This means that with a bit of reading and a little practice, you too can know just what to say and do in all sorts of circumstances.

Social savvy is not only a relatively simple skill to master, but also an important one. Our abilities in a whole range of areas are generalized based upon the social behaviors we exhibit. Whether you are interviewing for a new job, building your business, or seeking new social relationships, *manners matter.*

This book contains a number of etiquette guidelines to help you navigate some of the most common interactions. Please note that I use the word guidelines deliberately. Contrary to popular belief, etiquette is not about rules. I never speak of etiquette in terms of rules because for every etiquette rule, I can think of an exception (or two or three). Guidelines allow for variation. Guidelines understand that behaviors are situationally specific. For instance, while you would of course use a fork and knife when dining out at a fancy restaurant, you wouldn't think twice about using your fingers when eating pizza with your family at home. True social savvy means understanding not only what the etiquette guidelines are, but also when and how to apply them.

It is my hope that you will use this book in two ways. First, that you are enthralled enough to sit down with a refreshing drink and read it cover to cover. Second, that you will keep it on hand to refer to as etiquette issues arise. If you encounter etiquette emergencies outside of the topics covered in this book, please contact me via the Mannersmith website: www.mannersmith.com.

I hope you find this book both educational and entertaining.

chapter one

Public Places and Events

When you're at a public venue— whether it's a place of entertainment or a place of worship—your behavior affects others. Restaurants, the theater, the ballet, and sporting events are all places where we go to have a good time. But you need to make sure that your actions don't prevent others from having a good time, too. Similarly, in a house of worship, the way you act will affect others; in such a setting, it is important to show respect so as not to disturb those around you. What's more, knowing the proper etiquette associated with specific types of public places will make you feel more at ease when you're out and about.

Restaurants

Reserve Your Spot: If you're planning to dine out—whether with a romantic interest or a large gathering of friends—call in advance to make a reservation. By doing so, you'll avoid potentially long waits, which can become awkward when you're with a group or a date; plus, you don't want a bunch of hungry, cranky people on your hands.

Appropriate Attire: Consider the formality of the establishment when deciding what to wear. A ball gown in a roadside seafood shack is bound to attract negative attention, and a tube top paired with short shorts is bound to be a showstopper (and thus an evening ender) in an upscale restaurant.

While You Wait: Some establishments have impeccable timing and will seat you at the precise time of your reservation. Others are sometimes unable to control all of the unpredictable variables. Picking a fight with the maître d' is not a good way to set the tone for a night out and is certainly no guarantee for better service. Wait fifteen minutes before speaking with the person in charge, at which point you may politely ask how much longer it will be before your table is ready. After thirty minutes, approach again; a reputable establishment should offer you something for the inconvenience, such as a bottle of wine or a round of drinks on the house. If the maître d' does not readily volunteer such compensation, you may gently suggest that such a complimentary offering might make your wait more pleasant. If the maître d' is completely blasé, you should think twice before going back.

Where to Wait: Often, the maître d' will suggest that you wait at the bar until your table is ready. This is a smart move on the restaurant's part, as it encourages you to spend more money. If you wish to wait at the bar, by all means, do so. If not, try to move aside so that you aren't blocking the entrance.

Bar Basics: If you decide to wait at the bar, you aren't obligated to order a drink, though you may receive a number of looks from the bartenders, who count on tips for their income. If one person from your party orders a drink, everyone should. It is perfectly fine to order a soft drink, even if others are having alcoholic beverages. In finer establishments, if your table is called while you are still finishing your drink, a barkeep will collect your drinks and carry them to your table for you. In more casual places, you will be expected to carry your own drink. While bartenders usually prefer that you settle your tab before sitting down to dinner, you may ask the wait staff to include your bar balance in the final bill for the meal.

Take Your Seat: When a member of the wait staff or a gentleman in your party pulls your chair out for you, you should approach from the right side of the seat. When you are between the chair and the table, reach behind you and grab the seat before sitting down. The other person will further assist you by pushing the chair in; you should be pulling and guiding the chair as well.

Rights and Respect: When dining in a restaurant, pay attention to how your behavior may affect others. Smoking (which is not even permitted in some establishments), talking on a cell phone, blowing your nose excessively, speaking loudly, and using offensive language can prevent your companions as well as other patrons from enjoying their food.

Child Care: Establishments that cater to children are easily identified by their more relaxed atmosphere and their offerings of crayons, booster seats, and children's menus. Even at these welcoming venues, your kids must be kept under control at all times. Little ones playing in the aisles can create a work hazard for the wait staff and disturb other patrons. Should you decide to bring your children to a finer restaurant, you must be prepared to leave at any point their behavior begins to affect those around you. It's highly annoying for parents who have gone to the trouble and expense of hiring a baby-sitter so that they can have a quiet evening out to find themselves sitting next to a table filled with out-of-control children whose behavior goes undisciplined.

Corresponding Courses: Everyone at the table should order the same number of courses; it's awkward to have nothing in front of you while watching someone else eat, as is the reverse situation. Even if you aren't particularly hungry, you should match your companions course for course. If someone is hosting the meal, it is her responsibility to ensure that everyone knows how many courses to order. (If you're the one hosting the meal, this can be accomplished by mentioning what you intend to order for each course.) If no one is hosting, you should mention how wonderful everything looks on the menu and ask what everyone else is planning to have. If you aren't comfortable doing this, review the menu so that you are prepared with a selection for each course. If the waiter approaches you first, request your entrée and then observe what everyone else does. If others order an appetizer, you can say something like, "That sounds great. I think I will have the consommé too."

Corresponding Drinks: If others are ordering alcoholic beverages, you are not required to do so; however, you should order some kind of drink, whether it's soda or sparkling water. (For more information on etiquette and alcoholic beverages, see page 82).

"Garçon!" In the movies, it's common to see someone snap his fingers in the air and call out for the waiter. This type of commotion will certainly draw attention to you, but not in a good way. It is much better to make eye contact with your server to beckon him to your table. Or, if your waiter is terribly busy and you're having trouble getting his attention, ask another server to let your waiter know you need him. As a last resort, you may excuse yourself from the table to find the manager or maître d' and communicate your need for your waiter.

Let Them Work: The members of the wait staff work hard for their tips, so please let them earn their keep. Do not brush crumbs, stack plates, or pass glasses. You may think you're helping, but your movements can interfere with the flow of their work. Unless your server or busboy has specifically asked you to pass something, refrain from any such action.

Doggie Bag Dilemma: The portions at some restaurants are large enough to feed a small family. When you don't finish your meal, you should consider whom you are with before deciding whether or not to ask for a doggie bag. When you're on an interview, out with important clients, on a first date, or at a fine dining establishment, forgo the leftovers.

Pay Up: If you and your dining companions will be paying for your own meals—as opposed to splitting the bill evenly (see below)—there are two different approaches you may take. One method is to ask for separate checks, which must be done before you order (the nicer the restaurant, the less likely I am to ask the wait staff for separate bills, though this courtesy may be requested in even the most glitzy places). The second option is simply to figure out individual costs off a single check. In the latter scenario, each person's contribution should include the cost of her meal and drinks, her share of the tax and the tip, plus a few extra dollars (the reason for this last point is that members of a group consistently underestimate the cost of their fair share).

Even Steven: In some social circles, the check is divided evenly between members of the party, regardless of what each person has ordered. Before taking this approach, you should consider the financial means of your dining partners. The person working for the philanthropic organization who always orders a salad should not be put in the uncomfortable and financially straining position of having to subsidize the cost of the stockbroker's filet mignon. Be aware of and sensitive to others' situations.

Tossed Salads and Scrambled Eggs

If you are on a tight budget and order accordingly when dining out with friends, yet find that when the check comes you are expected to help finance your companions' meals, you need to speak up for yourself. You can use humor and say, "If I had known we were going to split the bill, I would have ordered the lobster, but since I am on a budget, I ordered the chicken. Here is the money to cover my share." Or, if you don't want to discuss your financial situation, you could say, "Oh, I am sorry, but I seem to have just enough here to cover my meal." Another option is to preempt the situation by taking the bill and asking your friends to put in an amount to cover their food and drink, plus tax and tip. If the money collected comes out a bit short, ask everyone to contribute another dollar or two. If this situation comes up frequently, you might consider taking one close friend aside and politely discussing the issue.

Always the Hostess: When hosting a meal at a restaurant, call ahead or arrive before your guests to review the menu and your table. You should also indicate whether or not you want alcohol to be served. Before your guests arrive, let the maître d' know that you don't want the bill to come to the table. Some establishments will ask that you leave a credit card at the beginning, while others are comfortable waiting until the end of the meal. Explain that after your guests are finished, you will walk them to the door and then return to settle the bill. Some of the finer restaurants will simply run your card and then mail you the receipt.

To Tip or Not to Tip: You are not obligated to tip the wait staff for poor service. That said, you are not allowed to leave nothing and just walk out. If the service was bad enough for you to even consider departing without giving a gratuity, you must speak with the management so that the server's behavior can be corrected.

Coat Connection: When a man is helping you with your coat, he will stand behind you, holding your coat open at the shoulders. Place your right hand and then your left hand in the appropriate sleeves. When both hands have found the sleeve openings, the gentleman will slide the coat up so that it rests comfortably on your shoulders.

For information dealing specifically with the etiquette of dining, see Chapter 4.

Patronizing the Fine Arts

Don't Dress Down: Most people would be appalled if they were served on paper plates at a fine restaurant, yet many of these same people think nothing of attending the theater in jeans. Part of what makes going to the theater fun is the ambience—to which the audience contributes. To make the event special for both you and those around you, take the time to dress up, at least a bit.

Special Seating: If you are going to a performance for which you don't have assigned seats, plan to arrive at such a time that will enable you to get the best view possible. If you have assigned seats, arrive at least fifteen to twenty minutes in advance of the scheduled start time to ensure that you are comfortably situated in your spot before the performance begins; if you arrive late, making your way to your seat can be disruptive to not only the rest of the audience, but the performers as well. You should know that many theaters and concert halls prohibit ushers from seating latecomers until there is a break in the performance.

Armrest Wrestling: Armrests come one per customer. Do not hog both. Your limbs and belongings should remain within your "territory" and control at all times. If you are claustrophobic or bigger-boned, try to purchase an aisle seat for your comfort as well as the comfort of those around you.

Let Them Pass: If others need to get in or out of your row after you've taken your seat, unless you are childlike in stature, you should rise to allow them to move by you. As you rise, your seat should fold up so that there is more physical space for the person to pass. Occasionally, it is easier to have everyone exit the row and then file back in the proper order.

Pardon Me: When it is necessary for you to leave your seat, make your exit as quickly and quietly as possible. If the performance is taking place, there is a good chance the people in your row will remain seated and you will need to navigate their limbs and belongings as you make a speedy retreat. Be aware of the people in your aisle, as well as the hair and shoulders of those in the row in front of you.

Quiet, Please: During a performance at the theater, opera, ballet, and similar settings, the only sounds should be coming from the stage; this means no talking while the singers, dancers, or actors are performing.

Cell Control: When attending a performance or the cinema, turn your cell phone off or switch it to vibrate. If you are truly concerned about a potential emergency, let the person know what theater you are going to and what seat you are in so that an usher can fetch you if necessary.

Consideration of Others: As you should in any public venue, be aware of how your behavior affects those around you. Wearing a big hat, unwrapping cough drops, sniffling or coughing excessively, and snapping gum (which you shouldn't be chewing anyway in public) are just some of the actions that are bound to interfere with other people's enjoyment of the show. Do your best to be a good neighbor; this includes limiting the number of times you get up from your seat.

Good Gracious, Gum!

I have a huge personal bias when it comes to gum. I actually worked in a candy factory, where we made all sorts of flavors. I love chewing gum. But you are going to have to get up pretty early in the morning to catch me doing it. Watching others chew gum is often a nauseating affair, and if they crack their gum, it can be nerve-racking. You should indulge in this activity only when you are alone.

Gotta Go: As any mother knows, a bathroom break is necessary before the start of a performance. You should also avoid consuming vast quantities of liquid before attending any kind of show. If nature calls once the show has begun, try to wait, if possible, for a break in the performance. If your bladder is reaching emergency status, you should evaluate the shortest escape route, make your apologies quickly (and quietly), and take care not to crush anyone's toes on your way out. Your return should be timed with a lull in the action to minimize disruptions.

Rock Concerts

Casual Clothing: When attending a rock concert, the "dress code" is obviously a lot more casual than what you should wear to the theater or opera. That said, neat, clean, and covered should be priorities.

Aerobic Exercise: It is expected at rock concerts that people will be singing along for some, if not all, of the songs. Singing is often accompanied by some dancing. Feel free to join in, but know where your extremities are at all times. Accidentally smacking your neighbor during your favorite tune is poor form.

On Your Feet: While you may prefer to take in the concert while seated, the fans in front of you may intend to dance the night away. If the majority of the people at the concert are standing, you might as well stand, too. However, if the rest of the concertgoers have taken their seats and only the three people in front of you are on their feet, exercising the utmost caution, you may politely ask if they would mind sitting for the next song or two.

Sporting Events

Go Team: Sporting events are a wonderful social outlet. Whether you're a hard-core devotee, a fair-weather fan, or a newcomer, you should recognize that sporting events are social happenings intended to be enjoyed, whether you're spending time with friends or meeting new people. And, depending on your job, attending such an event may be required for business.

Arm Yourself: If you're not a sporting loyalist, before you head to an event, take a little time to find out who the main or celebrity players are, as well as the basic rules for the particular sport (doing so is especially important if you'll be attending the event with business associates). Having this information will enable you to feel more comfortable, as well as allow you to engage in conversation with your fellow attendees. While asking a few questions can further your understanding of the game, as well as propel the conversation, pay attention to the way your companions respond before asking more. Some fans are thrilled to narrate a game for you, while others will quickly become annoyed.

Sportswear: Dress codes differ based on the sport. Do a little research to determine what is expected. In general, baseball, football, basketball, hockey, soccer, ice skating, and car racing tend to be casual events (be sure to take into account the climate of the arena when deciding what to wear). Golf, tennis, yachting, horse racing, polo, ballroom dancing, and croquet tend to be more formal events with specific attire prescribed.

An Edge over the Competition

Gentlewomen know that even if sports are not their thing, they should read the front page of the sports section every day. Timely sports information can serve as an easy conversation starter in both personal and professional situations.

Follow the Crowd: If you aren't an ardent fan and aren't sure what is expected of you, take note of everyone else's behavior. Some sports (such as golf) require absolute silence at certain times, while raucous cheering often prevails at other events. Be sure you aren't cheering (or even talking) during the quiet times! And, here too, those cellular telephones should be turned off or set to vibrate.

Tempting Fate: While you may be a fan of the visiting team, always be respectful of the home team. Crowds are notoriously unpredictable. If you are surrounded by fans from the other side, it may not be the best time to try out your new taunting cheer.

Places of Worship

Appropriate Attitude: As a guest in a place of worship, you should be respectful. This means refraining from speaking, chewing gum, answering your cell phone (the ringer of which should be off), or causing any other distraction during the service.

Purely Puritan: Unless you are absolutely positive that what you intend to wear is appropriate, select the most conservative ensemble in your closet. Many religious sites frown upon too tight, too plunging, too leggy, and too much skin. To be safe, your shoulders should be covered, shoes should be closed-toe, and panty hose should be worn (no bare legs). Unless you are familiar with the particular sanctuary, avoid pants, as in some places these are not considered acceptable. Jewelry should be modest, and religious symbols (other than those of the house of worship's faith) should be discreet or hidden.

Ask in Advance: If you are attending a service with which you are unfamiliar, ask those who have invited you what to expect. You should inquire about the type of service, the length of the service, and any specific rituals that will take place. If you are not comfortable asking someone or are unable to do so, search the Internet or visit your local library for some basic background information.

Be a Copycat: Out of respect, you should stand when the congregation stands and sit when the congregation sits. If you are not comfortable bowing, kneeling, or prostrating yourself when the congregation does so, you should remain seated (if the congregation is kneeling, however, sit forward in the pew so that the person behind you has enough space to kneel and pray).

Participation Protocol: If you are invited to participate in the service and would like to do so, you may. However, if you would prefer not to join in, you may politely decline. For example, if you are at a church and the worshipers are going to the altar for Communion, you have the choice of joining them or not (keep in mind that Communion is not a snack and has profound religious significance for those participating).

Money Matters: Attitudes toward bringing up the issue of money during religious services vary as widely as the services themselves. The leaders of some houses of worship feel it is their obligation to collect from the congregation when the members are gathered; others will make no mention of money during services. If a collection is taken, as a guest, you are not obligated to donate. However, if you have enjoyed the service or feel so moved, your contribution will be welcomed. You may donate on the spot or send a check later.

Stay or Go: Religious services vary in length. For a service that is less than an hour, you should make every effort to stay for the duration. When it comes to longer services, you should time your exit so that it doesn't interfere with the worshipers or the person conducting the service. Occasionally, there will be parts of a service when no one is allowed to enter or leave; usually, ushers are stationed at the doors during these times.

Funerals

Deepest Condolences: When you learn of some-one's death, it is your responsibility to contact the family and friends of the deceased to express condolence; if you can do so in person, that is best. Otherwise, you should do so by telephone, lastly by written word (for information regarding condolence notes, see page 159). Reasonable attempts should be made to attend the funeral service as a showing of support to those in mourning.

Spread the Word: As unpleasant as it may seem, unless the family has specifically asked otherwise, once you learn of someone's death, you should contact anyone else you feel should have this information. Most mourners are consumed with their loss and the funeral preparations and do not have time to call everyone. Furthermore, the mourners may not know all of the deceased's friends and acquaintances.

Saying Good-bye: The ceremonies with which we mark the end of someone's life are as varied as the ways we live. Some feature the deceased's favorite music as a celebration of life; others revolve around prayers and focus on death as a somber passing. If you will be attending a funeral involving a religion with which you are unfamiliar, take the time to find out in advance what will occur. If you are especially close to the mourners, you may ask them directly. Other avenues for research include the funeral home, the house of worship, your local library, and the Internet.

Say Something: Many people fear that they will say the wrong thing to those in mourning—so much so that they say nothing at all. Those who are grieving need to hear that you care. Typical expressions of condolence are "I am so sorry to learn of your loss" and "You and your family are in my thoughts and prayers."

Flowers and Food: To express sympathy, it is common to send something to the bereaved. The typical offerings are flowers and food. For followers of Buddhism and Hinduism, only flowers should be given. In Judaism, it is common that food be brought to the family. Both flowers and food are acceptable in Christianity and Islam.

Donations: In almost every situation, those in mourning will appreciate donations made to a charity in memory of the deceased. You may opt to do this instead of giving food or flowers. Often, the family will include in the obituary the names of suggested charities for those who would like to make a contribution. When individual charities have not been specified, consider the deceased's likes and activities when choosing an organization.

Attire: For most faiths, attire at a funeral consists of dark, somber colors. As is the case for religious services in general, clothing should be conservative. A woman should cover her arms, toes, and, in some instances, head. All jewelry should be kept to a minimum. Articles bearing symbols of another religion should be discreet or hidden.

Before and After: Members of some religions include other rituals in addition to the funeral to mark a person's passing. For instance, Catholics sometimes have a wake (typically a day or two before the funeral) for people to pay their respects. Family members and close friends will attend the burial; most mourners do not expect funeral attendees to witness the burial. Many do expect funeral attendees to pay their respects at a private home after the burial. Generally, those conducting the funeral service will provide information about the burial and condolence calls. Many Jewish people sit shivah at home for a week after the funeral; this is a time to remember the deceased and express sympathy to the mourners.

Attending a Wake

You should be aware that wakes often involve an open casket. If you are comfortable approaching the casket to pay your respects, you should do so. However, if you would rather not view the body, you are not obligated to do so. In such a situation, you should offer your condolences to the family, walk past the casket, and take your seat.

After the Fact: If you learn of someone's death after the funeral has taken place, you should still contact the family to express your sympathy. You should also send a note (people in mourning sometimes forget who has stopped by or called, but notes are often read in the quiet days, months, and even years that follow). If you have a fond memory of the individual, take the time to share it with the family.

The Year to Come: For many people who have lost loved ones, the whirlwind of activities surrounding the funeral consumes their attention. It is only in the subsequent weeks and months that the feeling of loss really hits. Be sure to call, visit, and write in the long days that follow, especially around holidays, birthdays, and anniversaries. Those in mourning will appreciate your kindness.

Removed Resources: If a member of your community has passed, and you were not close to the individual or the family, you may not feel comfortable attending the funeral. However, you can still provide support by performing tasks to assist the family. For instance, if you are a neighbor, you can offer to watch the house while the funeral is taking place or help to prepare and set up the food for after the ceremony. If the funeral is out of town, you can volunteer to pick up the mail or walk the dog.

chapter two

The Gracious Guest

Congratulations! You have just received an invitation for a party, a weekend getaway, or some other social activity. In addition to planning what to wear, you should review your guest obligations. What? A guest has obligations? Yes, indeed. The host should not be the only one doing the work. As is the case with any successful relationship, both parties need to contribute and do their part. And the more you live up to your end of the bargain, the greater the chance you'll be invited back!

The Basics

RSVP: Once upon a time, invitees understood that it was their obligation to respond to an invitation in a timely manner. But somehow, somewhere, people started to forget. So a gentle reminder in the form of an RSVP line began to appear with invitations. Then, in desperation, hosts began to include self-addressed stamped envelopes to make the lives of guests even easier. There is no excuse for ignoring the responsibility of responding. Do not wait for the RSVP date to arrive or, heaven forbid, pass before letting your host know whether or not you will be attending; the earlier you reply, the easier it is for the host to make all of the necessary arrangements. Never put the host in the position of having to track you down.

Always Inform: If you have any dietary restrictions, physical limitations, philosophical ideology, or religious beliefs that may affect your participation in the festivities, it is incumbent upon you to inform your host well in advance. Under no circumstances should you wait until the event to mention your need for special accommodations, as this will undoubtedly put some last-minute strain on the host.

No Additions: It is unacceptable to bring others to a party if they were not specifically invited or if you were not specifically told that you could bring guests. If you feel strongly about attending with another person (or bringing your children), you have the uncouth option of calling the hostess and pleading your case. Arriving with uninvited guests will ensure that you are not invited again in the near future. And showing up at an event with uninvited minors, especially infants, is a major faux pas.

Pets Prohibited: Unless your pets' presence has specifically been requested at a function, do not bring them along (even if it's an outdoor event). The host has enough to do without being confronted with the needs of your four-legged friends.

A Helping Hand: It is always a nice gesture to ask the host if there is anything you can do or bring. If the host accepts, be prepared to follow through. If the host declines, do not insist. Instead, save the idea, recipe, or game for your next soirée.

Be the Bearer of Gifts: When you've been invited to someone's home, you should present your host with a gift. Some typical options are wine, chocolates, homemade treats, and board games. If you plan to give flowers, it is best to send them (accompanied by a note of anticipation) so that they arrive on the morning of the event; that way, the host does not need to stop everything to attend to the flowers' needs in the middle of the gathering.

Giving and Receiving

Please note that when you bring something like a bottle of wine or a dessert, your host is not obligated to serve it. Presumably the host has spent a lot of time planning the menu. If your selection does not match, the host may prefer to save it for another time.

When in Rome . . . . If it's a costume party, wear a costume. If it's a dinner party, eat dinner. If it's a dance, get up and dance. Refusing to comply with the program will only draw negative attention to you.

Sing for Your Supper: When you attend a party or other gathering, you should be prepared to be entertaining. This doesn't mean you should perform your favorite aria while standing on the dining room table. However, you should arrive with some interesting topics of conversation to share with other guests (for some ideas, see page 109).

'Fess Up: If you break something (or cause the toilet to overflow) while you're a guest in someone's home, alert the host immediately, apologize, and offer to assist in the cleanup. (If the host indicates that he would prefer to handle the cleanup himself, respect his wishes.) Once the mess has been taken care of, you should offer to replace the item. (The host should decline, especially if the object was expensive.) While you want to make sure that the host knows how genuinely sorry you are, you should not cause the incident to become the main topic of conversation at the event. Let the matter go until afterward; then write an apologetic note and send a token gift, such as flowers.

Party Know-How

What to Wear: Women's dress codes have blurred and morphed so much over the past few years that it is difficult to know what to wear anymore. If you are uncertain about the appropriate apparel for an event, call the host for some guidance. If she tells you to wear "whatever," ask what she plans to wear and use her outfit as a benchmark. Keep in mind that it is always better to be overdressed than underdressed (for more information on attire, turn to the section that begins on page 105).

Footloose and Fancy-Free

When entering someone's home, there is always the possibility you will be asked to remove your shoes, whether the reason lies in a cultural practice or simply the desire to protect white carpets. (If the weather is messy, there is a good chance your host will request that you leave your footwear at the entrance.) If asked to remove your shoes, you should comply. So don't wear crazy-patterned socks that you wouldn't want anyone else to see or stockings with a hole in the heel. You never know if you'll be forced to reveal these otherwise hidden articles of clothing. (Often, hosts who are fussy about shoe removal will provide extra socks or slippers, but you can't count on this.)

Making Your Entrance: For structured affairs, such as seated dinners and showers, you should arrive at the appointed hour. For free-flowing events, such as a cocktail party or housewarming, you should arrive when you anticipate the party to be in full swing. The exact timing varies based upon social circle, economic standing, and geographic region, among other factors. As a general rule of thumb, unless you are the closest confidante of the host, you should not be the first person to arrive.

Meet and Mingle: Parties are great places to expand your social circle. Whether the setting is professional or personal, networking is always important, so take the initiative and interact with other guests. Even if you are shy, do not wait for someone to approach you. You might offer to help the host with the food, as this activity will give you something to do as well as facilitate conversation. "Would you like a cheese puff?" Or, you could look for someone else who isn't already engaged in a discussion and strike up a conversation. "How do you know the hostess?" is a safe question for getting the ball rolling.

Don't Be a Drama Queen: When attending an event, go in good spirits—even if you have to put on an act. Transforming someone's party into a stage for your latest drama is not fun for anyone involved. If you're in such a funk that you can't manage to fake a smile, stay home and pout by yourself.

Considerate Company: When you are at a party, be respectful of your host's home and belongings. Use coasters, and keep your feet off the furniture.

Here's Your Coat: Just as you shouldn't be the first person to arrive, unless you are the best friend of the host (or you're staying to help draw the red wine stains out of the ivory carpet), you shouldn't be the last to leave. Once your host has begun cleaning up and yawning, you have overstayed your welcome.

Thank You, Thank You: When leaving a party, you should always take the time to find and thank your host. Be sure to express what a wonderful time you had. If possible, you should also dash off a brief thank-you note when you arrive home. (While a hand-written note is preferable, at the very least you should e-mail or call the host within two days to say how much you enjoyed yourself.) Parties require a great deal of work, and recognizing your host's efforts will surely go a long way.

Staying Over

Communicate: Before you arrive, ask if there is anything your host would like you to bring; not every home stocks enough linens, towels, or pillows for visitors. Also, make sure that your arrival and departure times are convenient for your host.

Use Your Own Steam: Unless your host has offered to pick you up or make arrangements for you, you are responsible for getting yourself to your destination (you may, of course, ask your host for directions). The person with whom you're staying is under no obligation to pay for your transportation or retrieve you from the airport or train station.

Don't Go Empty-Handed: As is the case when you attend a party, you should arrive with a present for your host. While the typical hospitality gifts noted on page 29 are all appropriate, other options include fancy soaps, kitchen gadgets, something for the house, a coffee table book, or a specialty item from your hometown.

Pitch In: Make yourself useful by helping around the house; clear dishes, offer to pick up something at the store, or (if the host is agreeable) make dinner. In addition to assisting with daily household chores, take the host out for a nice meal at least once during your stay. If you're visiting for only one or two nights, there may not be time for a night on the town, but if you're staying any longer, dinner out is a requirement.

Be a Neat Freak: Always pick up after yourself when you're a guest in someone's home. Make your bed, keep the bathroom and room that you're sleeping in tidy, hang up wet towels, and don't let your personal items take over the residence.

Pay Your Way: If you are staying with someone for more than two days, or you visit more than three times a year, you should offer to contribute to the grocery bill and/or phone bill. Most hosts will decline, but it's important to offer.

Get with the Program: If you happen to be staying in a common room—perhaps a family room with a pullout sofa—plan your bedtime and waking time according to the schedule of the residents. If the members of the household retire early, follow suit, as they will most likely be rising early and in need of the space. If, on the other hand, they want to talk into the night, don't expect to turn out your lights too soon, but know that you will probably be able to sleep in a bit. If you are unsure about people's schedules, ask if there is a particular time that the space will be needed.

Make Yourself Scarce: It is important to give the host some private time during the day. Retire to your room for a nap, read a book, or take a long walk. Even better, spend an afternoon visiting local attractions. Invite the host, but be sure to give her the opportunity to decline. For instance, "I am off to see the Statue of Liberty today. If you would like to join me, you are more than welcome, but please don't change your plans on my account. I know how busy you are right now."

Use the Magic Three: When you are a guest in someone's home, make a special effort to use the magic words that show consideration and politesse: "please," "thank you," and "excuse me."

Ask First: Being a guest does not automatically grant you access to everything in the closets, refrigerator, and cabinets. Be sure to ask if you wish to use something belonging to your host.

Do Tell: If you have used up an item, such as toilet paper or orange juice, let your host know so that the item can be replaced. You can even bring up the issue in such a way that shows you intend to be helpful: "Claudia, if you tell me where you keep the toilet paper, I would be happy to replace the empty roll in the teal bathroom."

Strip: The bed, that is! Assuming that you didn't bring your own linens, when it's time for you to be on your way, leave the sheets and pillowcases—folded neatly—near the door of the room you were occupying or in the laundry room; fold the blanket and comforter, and place them at the foot of the bed. Check the area you were sleeping in and the bathroom for your personal effects, and be sure to tidy both spaces before your departure. If possible, you should also empty the wastepaper basket you were using.

Many Thanks: You may have already expressed your gratitude to the host in person, but don't stop there. Be sure to send a handwritten thank-you note once you have returned home. Remember, a gracious guest is a welcome guest.

Weddings

Don't Even Think About Wearing White: For weddings, engagement parties, bridal showers, and rehearsal dinners, leave the solid white attire to the bride.

By Invitation Only: Unless the invitation states "and guest" or "and family," you can presume that only the people specifically named on the invitation are invited. While you may think that others should be invited, the decision is not yours. If you have recently gotten married or engaged and your significant other was not invited, you may of course communicate your change in status and request that he be added to the list. Otherwise, do not ask to bring someone, as you will be putting the host in an awkward situation. For you singles out there, weddings are great places to meet potential significant others!

What to Give: The vast majority of brides and grooms register for items they would like to receive. While you are sure to make the couple happy with a gift from their wish list, you don't need to restrict yourself to the registry. Often, the most cherished and personal wedding gifts are those that have been selected with special thought.

What to Spend: Many people wonder how much money should be spent on a wedding gift. The answer varies according to many factors. First and foremost, you should consider your budget. Then you should consider your relationship with the couple getting married. Amounts vary widely based upon geographic region and social circle.

Pay for Postage: Whenever possible, send the wedding present in advance to the bride at her home or her parents' home instead of bringing it to the event. Gifts are easily misplaced during the festivities. Even a check should be mailed to ensure that the happy couple receives it. And, whenever possible, put the card for the gift inside the package or wrapping so that it doesn't get lost.

First-Year Fallacy: At some point, someone began a vicious rumor that a guest may wait up to one year to give the wedding couple a gift. This is simply r.ot an acceptable practice. Ideally, gifts should be given before the wedding.

To Give or Not to Give: The question often arises as to whether or not an invitation to a wedding carries with it a gift requirement if you don't attend. The answer is that wedding announcements and wedding invitations do not carry any such obligation. That said, I do recommend sending a card with your well wishes when you receive a wedding announcement, and giving at least a small gift if you have been invited to the wedding. But certainly you know your relationship with the bride and groom much better than I, and you will need to make the call as to what is most appropriate.

Ceremony and Celebration: I am always surprised to hear that some people feel attending the marriage ceremony is optional. This is the most important part of the wedding event. Skipping the ceremony and going to only the party is extremely tacky behavior. While the bride may not notice, other guests certainly will.

Arrive Before the Bride: This advice may seem highly obvious, but for some reason, there are always stragglers. Make every possible effort to arrive at the wedding ceremony prior to the bride's stroll down the aisle. Most guests arrive twenty to thirty minutes before the time indicated on the invitation. When deciding when to leave your home or hotel for the ceremony, account for traffic and possible parking issues—and then add a little extra time to be safe.

Lead the Way: At many wedding ceremonies, you will be escorted to your seat by an usher. A properly trained usher will greet you at the door and offer you his left arm, which will be bent at the elbow. You should then wrap your right hand around his elbow, and he will walk you to your seat. If you've been accompanied to the wedding, your date should follow immediately behind you.

Clicking Cameras: As long as you have not been informed that the ceremony site prohibits photography, you may take pictures during the processional and recessional—but that's it. At all other times during the ceremony, the only person who is allowed to be clicking away is the photographer hired for the event. The clicks, flashes, and sound of film rewinding can be highly distracting and, in some instances, may be viewed as disrespectful.

Watch Your Mouth: Weddings tend to be long functions, and you may exhaust your typical topics of discussion. However, you should not resort to making disparaging remarks about the bride, the groom, or the event. If you find the conversation at your table lagging, it might be a good time to get up and dance.

Sweet Endings: Hopefully, you are able to relax and enjoy the wedding festivities. If you've accepted the reception invitation, you should remain at the party until the cake has been cut. Once this ritual has taken place, you may leave if you must.

Gracious Good-byes: Before you depart, be sure to wish the wedding couple well, congratulate the families of the bride and groom, and thank the wedding hosts (i.e., those listed on the invitation).

Lost in the Mail: If you have not received an acknowledgment that your wedding gift was received within six weeks of the wedding (or within one month of the time you sent the present if you did so well in advance of the event), you should take action. Call the bride and say that you wanted to be sure your gift had arrived since you would be simply horrified if it had gotten lost in the mail and she thought you had not given her anything. If it turns out that the present was not received, you should call the store to track it down. If the gift was received, it is up to the bride to express her gratitude over the telephone and then write you a thank-you note once she has hung up.

chapter three

The Welcoming Host

As alluded to before, friendship is a reciprocal relationship. This means that there must be an exchange of give and take. Once you have been invited somewhere, it is up to you to return the invitation. Don't worry if the thought of having a full-blown, seven-course seated dinner in your cramped living space fills you with trepidation—there are many other options for entertaining.

Party Time!

Dollars to Doughnuts: Before you firm up any plans, consider your budget. You should never feel like you need to take out a mortgage to throw a party. There are many ways to be the hostess with the mostess without breaking the bank. From brunches and backyard barbecues to catered affairs and private restaurant rooms, your choices are almost limitless.

The Who's Who: When hosting a party or other gathering, invite a mix of people—those to whom you owe invitations, a few professional acquaintances, some members of your social circle, and even some close relatives. If you entertain only once in a blue moon, then your list will be longer, as you won't want to exclude anyone. But if you entertain frequently, you can be more selective for each individual event, as ultimately you will get around to including everyone.

Start Small: If you've never entertained before, don't begin with a cocktail party for a hundred people. Dinner for four is probably a better way to ease into the role of hostess. Then, with each success, you can plan bigger and bigger events.

Play to Your Strengths: If you're a gourmet chef, cook a fabulous dinner for your friends (for more information about dinner parties, see the section that begins on page 51). If you're a movie buff, invite people over for a showing with accompanying movie munchies. Restaurant aficionados might treat some friends to a fabulous meal at their new favorite place, sports fans might invite a group over to watch the big game, and microbrew connoisseurs might offer a tasting.

Come on Over: Once you've started making the plans for a gathering, you'll want to invite your guests. (For information regarding invitations, see page 50.)

Setting the Stage: Well in advance of the party, take a good look at the rooms in which you will be entertaining your guests. Make sure that there are places for people to sit comfortably and rest their drinks (have plenty of coasters and cocktail napkins on hand). You might also want to remove any precious or fragile items.

Modulate the Music: Background music can add ambience to a gathering. Select tunes that will set the tone you wish to achieve, and keep the volume low so as not to interfere with guests' conversations. When you are ready for guests to leave, one of the signals you can use to get the point across is to turn off the music.

Warm Welcome: Whenever possible, you should greet your guests at the door, take their coats, and direct them toward the action. If a guest does not know others at the get-together, take a moment to introduce him to someone he has something in common with, get the conversation started, and then excuse yourself (for information on how to make an introduction, see page 108). If the weather has taken a turn for the worse, be prepared to accommodate wet umbrellas, coats, and boots; towels and directions to the nearest mirror may also be necessary. When your attention is needed elsewhere, ask another guest to help greet. This is a great activity for someone who is a bit shy.

Fabulous Footsies: Whether you're trying to protect your floors or it's simply a house rule, if you want guests to remove their shoes at the door, you should provide slippers or socks for their use. Most guests will not anticipate the need to remove their footwear and may be caught off guard by your request. Having slippers or socks on hand will help prevent anyone with hosiery or foot issues from feeling uncomfortable.

Party Participation: As the host, you should take part in the party as much as possible, as opposed to spending most of the time in the kitchen away from your guests. To help accomplish this, do as much preparation as you can in advance; you might want to serve some hors d'oeuvres and dishes that you can put together the day before and then simply stick in the oven just before the event. Another option is to hire help. This doesn't necessarily mean retaining the services of a pricey caterer's wait staff. A neighborhood teenager or college student may be able to help. Be creative!

Refreshments for All: If you will be serving alcohol, be sure to offer nonalcoholic beverages as well. Sparkling water and soda are some possible options.

Bar Basics: Just as you plan the menu for the food, you should plan the menu for the bar. When hosting smaller parties, you can perform the role of bartender. For larger parties, hire a bartender so that you have time to interact with your guests. Limiting your alcoholic offerings to beer and wine is a perfectly acceptable approach that will make your job easier. If you want to include mixed drinks, consider offering only one or two specific kinds so that you don't need to spend the whole time making cocktails. If you plan to play bartender, be sure you know what to do. At the very least, purchase a cocktail guide and a bar mixing set. Even better, sign up for an adult education bartending course!

Great Glasses: If you already possess a plethora of barware and stemware, wonderful. If not, attempt to acquire at least a set of tumblers and some all-purpose stemware. For those of you who aspire to the finer things in life, here are some glasses that you might want to have on hand.

Bordeaux wine glass: This red wine glass is large in size to allow for a greater amount of aeration (Bordeaux region wines need contact with the air). In addition, these wines have more sediment particles than others, and the larger glass allows these pieces to sink to the bottom.

Burgundy wine glass: Boasting a balloon-shaped bowl, this red wine glass tends to be smaller than the Bordeaux. This is because Burgundy wines have less sediment and are formulated to be consumed without decantation or aeration.

White wine glass: This glass tends to be narrower at the lip than the stemware designed for red wine. The shape allows for the delicate bouquet to concentrate toward the top of the glass.

Water goblet: As the name suggests, this piece of stemware is designed to hold water. Generally, it is slightly larger than the wine glasses.

Champagne coupe: Legend has it that this style of champagne glass was modeled after the breast of Helen of Troy, and that the design was later updated by Marie Antoinette. Regardless of whether the stories are true, the design allows for the rapid loss of precious bubbles and is eschewed by champagne aficionados.

Champagne flute: This tall, thin glass is elegant with a purpose. The design allows for the bubbles to catch on the sides of the glass, roll down to the exact center of the bottom, and then rise, single file, to the surface. The better the design and the better the champagne, the better the behavior of the bubbles.

Liqueur: Smaller than a traditional wine glass, this piece of stemware is generally used to serve cordials and eaux-de-vie.

Pilsner: This tall, thin glass was designed for Pilsner beers to help accentuate the color and taste that distinguish them from other types of beer. Today, most people use this glass to serve any kind of beer.

Highball: This tall, thin tumbler-style glass (i.e., sans stem) is used for cocktails mixed with either soda or water, as well as for soft drinks.

Double old-fashioned: Shorter and wider than the highball, this tumbler-style glass is used for drinks that contain only alcoholic ingredients; often, these drinks are served on the rocks.

Martini glass: This stylish glass is easily recognized by its slender stem, angular bowl, and wide rim. As its name suggests, this is the glass you would use to serve martinis.

Brandy snifter: Usually boasting a very short stem and a very round bowl, this glass is designed to be cupped in the palm of the hand. Brandy is best enjoyed warm, and the heat from the drinker's hand helps to warm the liquid.

Bordeaux

Burgundy

White wine

Water

Champagne coupe

Champagne flute

Liqueur

Pilsner

Highball

Double old-fashioned

Martini

Brandy snifter

Never a Dull Moment: Savvy hosts know how to keep a party moving along. While everyone may roll their eyes at the mention of a parlor game, any hostess worth her weight in mousse knows the importance of continuous interaction at a social gathering. The activity can be a tried-and-true standard such as charades, a rousing round of sing-along tunes with someone playing piano, or even a make-your-own-sundae bar. You know your guests better than anyone, so select some activity that you think they'll enjoy should the party need a boost.

Game Time

One of the activities I use as an icebreaker is a trivia game. Each guest writes out a fact about himself that no one in the room knows. These bits of information (which may be written on small note cards or pieces of paper) are then collected into a pile (you might opt to use a basket for this purpose). Each participant pulls a card from the pile and has twenty minutes to speak to as many guests as possible in an attempt to find the person whom the card describes. When twenty minutes are up, the host asks everyone to come together and calls upon an extroverted guest to read his card and introduce his match. The match then reads what is on her card and introduces her match until everyone has been covered.

Subtle Signals: It is up to you to give your guests cues. You must orchestrate when they should drink, eat, mingle, and, yes, even leave. Delightful parties are ones where the guests want to stay all night. Hosts wish their guests a good evening while everyone is still having fun instead of waiting for the party to die. "So glad you could come!" "It would not have been the same without you!"

Parting Gifts: Although this is certainly not a requirement, many hosts like their guests to leave with a little something (preferably not a piece of Grandmother's silver). Favors need not be grand. They are merely token gifts that let your guests know how much you appreciated their presence. Chocolates and other edible treats are some appropriate options.

Secret to Success: There is nothing that has a greater effect on a gathering's success than the attitude of the host. When the host is calm and attentive, the guests will relax and enjoy their time together.

Issuing Invitations

Setting the Tone: It is from the invitation that guests get their first impression of the event to come. Thus, the invitation should reflect the tone of the gathering. The fancier the party, the fancier the invitation. You might invite friends to a casual Sunday brunch via telephone, ask people over for drinks after work via e-mail, or request the pleasure of others' company at a sit-down dinner via the postal service.

Putting It in Writing: When it comes to written invitations, there are a number of options from which you may choose. You may handwrite them on stationery, purchase preprinted ones with blank spaces where you fill in your specifics, or order customized invitations. There are varying degrees of formality for all three approaches. Keep in mind that the level of formality is conveyed not only by the style of the invitation, but by the choice of words as well.

Crucial Contents: When extending an invitation, you must include your name; the date, time, and location of the event; the purpose of the event (birthday celebration, dinner party, cocktails, brunch, etc.); the date by which you wish your guests to RSVP; and the name of the person to whom guests should RSVP, along with the corresponding mailing address, telephone number, or e-mail address. If the party is being held in someone's honor, that person's name should obviously be featured as well. A line regarding the expected attire may also be included in the invitation.

Enough Notice: For a casual get-together, you might extend the invitations the week before, but for a formal event, you might issue them as early as months in advance. The telephone and e-mail are generally used for functions that are one to three weeks away. Mailed invitations are generally employed for events one to two months away. If your event involves out-of-town guests, you should issue the invitations well in advance (two months is advisable) to be sure that the nonlocal folks have time to make the necessary travel arrangements.

The Dinner Party

Treats to Tide You Over: You may have invited your guests for dinner, but that doesn't mean only dinner should be served. Be prepared to offer your invitees hors d'oeuvres and beverages when they arrive (these should be served in a different room than where the actual dinner will be held). Guests do not always show up on time, and you don't want your prompt friends to be chewing on their fingernails while they wait. Plus, serving hors d'oeuvres and drinks in the living room allows your guests to mingle before sitting down to the meal. Appropriate offerings include anything from veggies and dip or cheese and crackers to warm passed hors d'oeuvres. (Budget minimalists might choose to put out some nuts and dried fruits instead.)

Pièce de Résistance: Giving a dinner party without offering dessert is like buying a wonderful present and not wrapping it—it's unfinished. Dessert is the lasting impression guests will take away from your meal. In fact, even if dinner was a disaster, a tasty treat at the end can ensure that your friends leave with a favorable impression of the evening. You might wish to give your guests a little time to relax between the entrée and dessert by having them retire to another room. If you wish to serve dessert at the dining table, this will give you the opportunity to reset. You also have the option of bringing the sweets to your guests once they are comfortably settled in another spot.

Adornments for Ambience: The phrase "party decorations" often brings to mind images of streamers and balloons. While these are fun embellishments for kids' birthday parties, a dinner party requires something more subtle and sophisticated, such as flowers and candles. Make sure that your decorations enhance your table without being distracting or disrupting guests' views of one another. And stay away from blooms with powerful scents, as these can interfere with people's enjoyment of the food.

Musical Chairs: A good host knows that where people sit for a dinner is just as important as what they are about to eat. While there are formal guidelines for seating, unless you are entertaining royalty, interests and attraction should guide your designations. Married and committed couples should not be seated next to each other, unless they are engaged or newlyweds, in which case they should be seated side by side. When possible, many hosts also alternate seating by gender. However, this is only a guideline, not a requirement. (For information on how to set the table, see page 54.)

A Formal Affair: In formal situations, the following seating configuration is used. The host sits at the head of the table with the host's significant other at the foot. The guest of honor, if there is one, sits to the host's right. The guest of honor's significant other sits to the right of the host's significant other. The second most important guest is seated to the left of the host's significant other, while this important person's significant other is seated to the left of the host. The table is filled in this way based upon rank, as well as gender. Ideally there is an even number of people, and whenever possible, the configuration should alternate between male and female.

Cultural Variations

You should know that in many Asian cultures, the guest of honor is seated facing the door. In some eastern European cultures, the guest of honor is seated at the middle of the table. Lastly, there are other cultures in which the guest of honor sits facing the most beautiful view of the room.

Places, Everyone: Place cards are nifty devices for helping guests to find their seats. They can be elaborate (guests' names written in calligraphy on handpressed paper tags attached by ribbon to gilded flowers) or simple (neatly written on tented cards). The place cards should match the tone and theme of your party. If creatively designed, they might double as party favors.

Setting the Table

Need-to-Use Basis: You should set out only dishes, utensils, and glasses that guests will actually be using during the meal. So if you're not serving a soup course, don't include a soup spoon in the place settings.

Center Stage: The dinner plate belongs at the center of the place setting. When the entrée is being plated in the kitchen (as opposed to being served from platters at the table), there are three options. The first is to include the dinner plate in the initial setting, but then remove it when the time comes to serve the meal. The second is to put out a slightly larger plate known as a charger, which is simply a place holder (you would not eat food off this dish). The third is to leave the space where the plate will ultimately be placed empty at the start (this approach, however, makes the table seem a bit naked, and thus is rarely employed for formal meals). The soup and salad dishes may be set upon the dinner plate or the charger when served.

Forks: The forks are set to the left of the plate in the order that they will be used. The fork that will be needed first should be farthest from the plate.

Napkin: In formal place settings, the napkin is generally placed to the left of the forks (this enables you to pick it up without disrupting your flatware). In less formal situations, the napkin may be placed under the forks or on top of the plate. Under no circumstances should you stuff a napkin in a water goblet.

Knives: With the exception of the butter knife, the knives belong to the right of the plate, arranged in the order that they will be used. The knife that will be employed first should be situated farthest from the plate. Place each knife so that the serrated edge faces the plate.

Soup Spoon: If you are having soup, the soup spoon should be placed to the right of the knives.

Dessert Utensils: When you include the dessert spoon and fork in your place setting from the start, you may situate them directly above the plate in a horizontal position. The dessert spoon should be the uppermost utensil, with its handle to the right, and the dessert fork should be situated just below it, with the handle to the left.

Bread Plate: The bread plate should be situated above and slightly to the left of the forks. Place the butter knife (if you have enough for everyone) horizontally on top of the bread plate, with the handle to the right.

Glasses: The glasses are placed above the knives and arranged so that they curve downward (see page 56 for their placement at a formal table). Were you to offer champagne as well, the champagne glass would be positioned farthest to the right with respect to the other glasses. (Note that when the formal toasting takes place after the main course, the champagne glasses are not set, but rather filled and presented prior to dessert.) For formal dinners, the coffee cup and saucer are not put out until dessert is served (at which point they would be placed above and to the right of the dessert plate). At a more casual meal, the coffee cup and saucer may be set at the beginning.

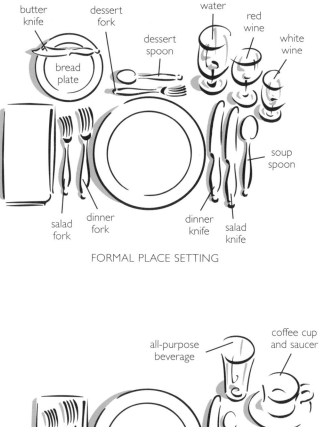

FORMAL PLACE SETTING

INFORMAL PLACE SETTING

Overnight Guests

Please Come: When inviting someone to your home as an overnight guest, discuss the logistics in advance. Some of the topics you'll want to cover include specific dates and times (arrival and departure), travel arrangements (while you should give directions and advice, you are not required to provide transportation), where the guest will be staying within your home (especially if in a shared or common space, as opposed to a dedicated guest bedroom), and anything you need your visitor to bring (a towel, for instance, if you are short on linens).

Standard Sleeping: If you have a dedicated guest room, wonderful; if your guest room is your couch, that's fine, too. Either way, guests should be made as comfortable as possible. Ideally, you should provide sheets, a pillow (preferably two, if you are equipped to do so), and a blanket; again, if you are unable to outfit your guest with any of these items, communicate this information ahead of time so that she may bring the necessary articles from home.

Bathroom Basics: You should provide your guest with a bath towel, a hand towel, and a washcloth. When she arrives, show her where everything is in the bathroom and let her know what is available for use. If there is a trick to turning on your shower, or if the toilet handle needs to be jiggled just so, now is the time to share this information. If there are items you don't want your guest to use (or see, for that matter), remove them ahead of time.

Appreciated Extras: There are a number of additional items that will enhance your guest's stay. Providing these little extras does not take much effort, but will go a long way toward making your guest feel at home.

+ travel- or sample-size shampoo, conditioner, and soap, which may be arranged in a basket in the bathroom
+ an extra toothbrush (in case your guest forgets to pack one), toothpaste, adhesive bandages, and headache relief—all in a spot readily accessible to your guest
+ reading materials—favorite books, recent magazines, and tourist materials are all options
+ a reading light, situated so that your guest can conveniently turn it on and off without needing to get out of bed
+ a glass of water at bedtime—and a spot to rest it near the bed (don't forget a coaster)
+ an alarm clock
+ a single flower in a bud vase beside the bed— always a charming decorative touch (as long as your visitor isn't allergic)

Stock Up: Prior to your guest's arrival, ask if there is anything she prefers to drink and eat, including any favorite snacks. Having some familiar food items on hand will make her stay more pleasant.

Place to Unpack: Again, if you have a guest room, great. If your guest will be staying in a common area, clear a space for her personal belongings and make some room in a closet for any hanging items.

Clear Communication: Once the guest has had a chance to settle in, you should talk about the expectations you each have for the visit. Any planned activities or events, typical meal times, and even what time everyone should be up the next day should all be discussed. Communication, or the lack thereof, can make or break a visit.

Special Schedule: Since you do have a guest, you will need to adjust your schedule a bit. While making your guest comfortable is a priority, you are not her servant. If she wanted to be waited upon hand and foot, she should have stayed at a luxury hotel.

House Rules: If there is anything regarding how things are done in your home that is important to you, you should educate your guest about these processes up front in an open and clear manner. For example, if plastic and glass bottles should be discarded in the recycling bin, and if crumbs or food that's being thrown out should go into the garbage disposal as opposed to the trash can, let your guest know.

Keep a Light On: It is a good idea to put a night-light on in the hall or simply leave a hall light on, in case your guest gets up in the middle of the night; you don't want her groping around in the dark in unfamiliar territory.

Pet Protocol

Forewarn of Fur: If you have a pet, when inviting guests to your home, let them know. Whether they have an allergy or simply an aversion, people should not be shocked when they arrive to find that human beings are not the only residents.

Greeting Guests: While you may enjoy receiving greetings from your pet when you walk in the door, not all of your visitors will want a sniff and a kiss. Try to contain your pet during the initial introductions.

Best Behavior: Having guests over can be exciting for not only you, but your pet as well. To avoid any overzealous behavior that might be upsetting to visitors, you may want to tucker out your pet ahead of time and then sequester him while you have company.

Managing Meals: Fluffy may regularly walk on your kitchen counters, but try to avoid having her do so when guests are over (especially if they're invited for dinner). You should also refrain from letting Fido lick your hand as you're preparing food. And no guest should be forced to endure a pet begging at the table.

chapter four

Gracious Dining

Ah, the elegance, the allure, the intimidation of a well-set table. While everyone knows the etiquette police are not waiting to take you away if you use the wrong fork, many people are still filled with trepidation when dining at a social gathering. In this world of fast food, plastic utensils, and meals-in-a-mug, it's no wonder we are out of practice. The best way to be more at ease when dining out is to educate yourself. The rules are not difficult, and the more you know, the more comfortable you'll be—and the more you'll enjoy yourself.

Utensil Usage
and Silent Signals

Differences in Style: There are actually two different approaches when it comes to dining with forks and knives: American and Continental (although the latter term is a reference to western Europe, the method can be found worldwide).

American Dining: In the American style of dining, the tines face up once the food has been speared, and the fork is held in the right hand when transporting food from plate to mouth. When food needs to be cut, the fork is transferred to the left hand, tines down, and the cut is made with the knife in the right hand. Once the mission has been accomplished, the knife is placed in the resting position on the plate (see illustration on page 64), and the fork is transferred back to the right hand.

Continental Dining: In Continental dining, the fork is held in the left hand with the tines down, while the knife stays in the right hand. There is no switching of hands, and the knife is held in between cuts rather than returned to the plate. The fork is turned toward the mouth (tines still down) using the wrist. Among some circles, the Continental style of dining is viewed as the "higher" method, due to the graceful motion of the fork and the relative quietness that results from keeping the knife in one's hand as opposed to constantly placing it on the plate.

Consistency Counts: It doesn't matter whether you practice the American or Continental style of dining, as long as you stick with one throughout the meal.

Outside In: Properly set utensils are placed in the order in which they will be used. Generally, you are safe to start with the utensils farthest from your plate, and then work your way in as you progress from course to course. If you are unsure, watch to see which utensil your host uses. Often, your dessert fork and spoon will be stationed above your plate (see the illustration of a formal place setting on page 56). If these utensils are not moved by your server when your entrée is cleared, you may bring the fork down to your left and the spoon down to your right at this point.

Cutting Edge: Knives should always be placed with the serrated edge facing toward your plate. The sharp edge faced out is seen as a sign of open hostility toward your neighbor.

Never the Twain Shall Meet: Once a utensil has touched food, it must never touch the table's surface again.

Taking a Breather: By placing your utensils in the proper position, you send a silent message to your companions and any wait staff, letting them know when you are simply resting and when you are finished with your meal. Think of your plate as the face of a clock. In both the American and Continental styles of dining, a state of resting is indicated by placing the top of the knife at twelve o'clock and the base of the handle at four o'clock (with the serrated edge facing in); meanwhile, the top of the fork should be placed at twelve o'clock and the base of its handle at eight o'clock. The only difference between the American and Continental resting positions is that the fork tines face upward in American dining but downward in Continental.

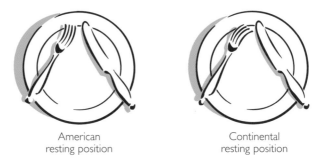

American
resting position

Continental
resting position

Finished: If you dine in the American style, to indicate that you are finished with your meal, situate the knife just as you would for resting, but place the fork (tines may be up or down) alongside the left edge of the knife. In Continental dining, you have a choice; you may either place the fork and knife as you would in the American style (though the tines must be down), or you may place the fork (tines down) and knife so that they form an X.

American
finished position

Continental
finished position

Spooning Soup: Unlike most other foods, when you eat soup, you move the utensil away from your body before bringing it to your mouth. Start by placing your soup spoon in the soup at the point closest to you, and collect soup on the spoon as you move the utensil away from you; then, raise the spoon directly over the bowl and bring it to your mouth while keeping your back straight and leaning in slightly from your hips. Silently sip the soup (no slurping, please) from the side of the spoon. This should all be done in a single, fluid (pun unintended) motion.

Soup Suspension: Because of the difference in the way it is served, soup has its own rules when it comes to utensil placement. When you are resting (as opposed to being finished), place the soup spoon in the cup or the bowl, with the handle at about three o'clock.

Soup to Nuts: When soup is served in a cup with a saucer, to indicate that you are finished, place the spoon on the saucer behind the cup, with the bowl of the spoon to the left and the handle to the right. When soup is served in a bowl on a plate, if the rim of the plate is wide enough, you may place the spoon on the plate behind the bowl, again with the bowl of the spoon to the left and the handle to the right. If the

Soup spoon
resting position

Soup spoon
finished position

soup is served in a bowl without a plate or with a plate that is too small, the finished position is the same as the resting position, with the spoon inside the bowl.

Salad Schedule: When dining in the American style, your salad will be served before the main course. In finer establishments, you'll be provided with a salad knife (along with the usual salad fork) to help you cut the lettuce leaves into a manageable bite size. In Continental dining, the salad is generally served after the meal. Continental diners typically fold their salad leaves rather than cutting them.

Bon Appétit

Simon Says: I liken gracious dining to a grown-up game of Simon Says. Your host is "Simon." Until this leader does—or tells you to do—something, you must wait. Simon is generally the person who did the inviting or the person who will be paying for the meal. If you are at someone's home, the homeowner is Simon. If you are out at a restaurant, the person who coordinated the event is Simon. If you are with a group of friends at a restaurant and each of you will be covering your own costs, you are your own Simon, but you must watch what the other Simons at your table are doing.

Mine vs. Yours: One of the bigger challenges when dining with others is figuring out which bread plate is yours and which water glass is yours. My favorite memory trigger for accomplishing this feat is "B.M.W.," which in this instance stands for "Bread, Meal, and Water"; when you're sitting at your place setting, this is the order in which these articles should appear from left to right (the same way you'd read these letters).

Napkin Notice: You should not take your napkin from your place setting until the host does so. When prompted, unfold your napkin completely, refold it in half, and place the fold at your knees with the other two corners at your hips. This allows you easy access to one corner at a time to dab your lips and wipe crumbs from your mouth. If you are the host, or in a situation where there is no host, take your napkin from your place setting once everyone is comfortably seated.

Food to Face: Proper posture is an essential aspect of gracious dining. Sit with your back straight, leaning in slightly from your hips, and raise your food over your plate up to your mouth. Do not slouch or bring your face to your food.

Elbows off the Table: In America, we rest our hands in our lap when we are not using them to eat. Just about everywhere else in the world, hands are kept at all times where everyone can see them.

Same Settings: Your place setting must match every-one else's, so you are not at liberty to rearrange it. While you may be tempted to bring your bread plate closer or move your water glass to your left, you must refrain from doing so. The purpose of this arrangement is not merely to create an aesthetically pleasing table, but to enable other diners and the wait staff to easily identify what belongs to you versus your neighbor.

Exceptions to the Rule

A great etiquette debate involves plate rotation and adjustment. There are those who say that once a plate has been set, you may not move it at all. Others, myself included, allow for slight movements in certain situations to prevent a more unfortunate occurrence from happening. If the plate is precariously close to the edge, you are allowed one adjustment so that it doesn't end up crashing onto the floor or falling into your lap. If the server positioned the plate so that the main portion of your entrée is farthest from you, making it difficult to cut, you are also allowed one adjustment.

Group Gratitude: You may find yourself in a situation where the host chooses to recite a prayer before eating. If you feel comfortable praying, you may of course do so. If you would rather not, simply bow your head out of respect.

The Green Light: You should not begin eating until the host commences or signals you to do so (the only substance that may pass your lips before you have been given the go-ahead is water). The host may wait until everyone is served or—if the group is large or the course is hot—tell those who have food to start so that their meals don't get cold (the latter is the more gracious approach). If you start before everyone is served, eat slowly; you should still have food in front of you when the others receive their meals. When you are out with friends in a situation where there is no host, you should wait until everyone has been served before digging in; and, in this situation, if you are one of the diners who doesn't yet have her dish, you should tell the others to go ahead and eat. This is the considerate thing to do.

Roll Roulette: The person sitting closest to the bread basket is the one who should set it off on its journey around the table. If you're at a gathering with a host, the host will give the signal as to when to start the bread; when dining out without a host, you may start the bread after everyone has been seated, though I prefer to wait until everyone has ordered. If you find yourself closest to the bread, pick up the basket and verbally offer a piece to the person sitting to your left (do not put your fingers on the bread itself). The recipient of your offer should then take a piece and put it on her bread plate while you continue to hold the basket. You may then take a piece for yourself and pass the basket to your right. Each person thereafter takes her own piece and continues passing to the right. Bread is the only item that is initially offered left and then passed right.

Feels Like Butter: When you are taking some butter from a shared butter dish, put it on your bread plate—not directly on your bread. If you have your own butter knife, use it; otherwise, use the shared butter knife or fork accompanying the butter dish.

Crummy Behavior: The proper way to eat bread is not what people usually expect. Simply tear off a bite-size piece (see definition on page 70), place the rest of the bread back on your bread plate, butter only the piece that you are about to eat, and then pop that piece into your mouth. While this method does create a good deal of crumbs, the result is an expected and accepted one.

Bite Size: When dining with others, you should take ladylike bites. The true measure of the appropriate bite size is the amount of food that you can chew three or four times and swallow without choking. (Since you are forbidden to talk with your mouth full, taking modest-size bites will allow you to participate in the conversation more often.) The more important your company, the smaller your bite size should be. First dates and job interviews require that you take tiny bites, whereas dinner with friends allows for a slightly larger bite.

See Food: Yes, this is an old elementary school joke, but while children under the age of ten might find chewed food to be hilarious, adults do not. Chew with your mouth shut. If you are having trouble closing your mouth, perhaps you should revisit the definition of bite size.

Incoming and Outgoing: When food is served to you, as opposed to your serving yourself from platters at the table, it is brought to you over your left shoulder. This is important to know so that you can lean slightly to your right when your dish arrives. Plates are cleared from the right side of your place setting, so when someone approaches to take away your dish, lean slightly to the left to make the task easier. (Note that some European-style venues clear from the left, so pay attention.)

Counterclockwise Circulation: Platters and other serving dishes should travel around the table in a counterclockwise direction; in other words, pass to your right. This one-way-only movement prevents traffic jams. What's more, the counterclockwise motion allows you to take the platter with your left hand, leaving your right hand free to serve. Since most people are right-handed, this permits the majority of people to serve themselves more easily, making mishaps less likely to occur. (Lefties, hang in there; you win out during cocktail parties [see page III].)

Taste Test: You should always taste your food before adding extra seasoning. You have no idea how heavy-handed the chef is with spices, and the food may be flavorful enough already. In addition, if you are dining in someone's home, there is a good chance the person who prepared the meal will be insulted if you do not sample the cooking before trying to alter the taste.

Manners and Moving Ahead

There is an apocryphal story about an executive who, when up for a promotion, was invited to lunch with the CEO. When the food came, the executive salted his food before tasting it. The CEO denied the promotion on the basis that the employee took action before gathering information to evaluate the situation. The tale just goes to show the impact that good manners—or rather a lack thereof—can have on your life.

Joined at the Hip: The salt and pepper shakers should be passed together, even if a fellow diner asks for only one or the other. There are a number of reasons behind this practice. One stems from the fact that the salt and pepper shakers are often the smallest items on the table and can easily get lost if not positioned together. Another reason is that in the olden days salt was very expensive, and it was viewed as gauche to specifically request something that was known to be dear; therefore, people were trained to ask only for the pepper, knowing that the salt, too, would be passed. Note that in some cultures it is believed that the absorbent qualities of salt draw in bad vibes and if you hand someone the salt directly, you are passing along your negative emotions. Thus, if someone asks for the salt but then does not extend her hand to take it from you, place it down on the table so she may pick it up directly.

Condiments That Complement: While you should taste your food before adding salt or pepper to it, condiments may be added at any time, since the decision to do so is usually based on personal preference as opposed to whether or not the food needs a little something extra. You already know if you like butter on your bread, sour cream on your baked potato, or lemon on your fish.

Sharing Servings: This practice should occur only with someone you know well. If you plan to split an order, let your wait person know so that the food can be brought out on two separate plates, preventing you from needing to do the work—often a messy task—at the table.

Cool It: If your soup is too hot to eat, you should allow it to sit and cool—do not blow on it. This is a good opportunity for you to practice your delightful dinner conversation.

Concise Cutting: You should cut only the piece of food you are about to eat. This rule of etiquette stems from practicality, preventing hot food from cooling down too quickly.

Purist vs. Mixing: It is acceptable to take a bit of meat and a bit of vegetable on your fork and eat them in the same mouthful, as long as you don't overdo your polite bite size. However, mixing your entire meal on your plate may cause too much attention to be focused on you and your eating habits.

UFO's and "IFO's": Unidentified flying objects and identified fallen objects should be handled with care. When you're at a restaurant, once a utensil hits the floor, it is no longer in your domain; you should signal a wait person to bring you a new utensil. If you're at someone's home, pick up the utensil and take it to the kitchen to be washed before use. A gracious host will jump up to help. If he is otherwise occupied or you're attending a casual gathering, you may wash the utensil yourself.

Spills and Thrills: Some find it challenging to make it through an entire meal without spilling something or dropping a morsel of food. If a piece of lettuce falls from your plate onto the table, you should discreetly pick it up and put it back on your plate (not to be eaten). If it falls on the floor, it is out of your domain—let it be. If you knock over your wine glass, cover the spill with your napkin. At a restaurant, the wait staff will take it from here. When you are in someone's home, ask the host what you can do. If he says not to do anything, allow him to clean the spot.

Sealed with a Single Kiss

If you wear lipstick, watch for the kiss mark on the rim of your glass after you've taken your first sip. You should continue to drink from this spot so that there is only one mark on the glass; marks all the way around the rim make for an unappealing sight.

Fast Finish: If you notice that you always finish your meal before everyone else, it's time to slow down—you should be eating at the same pace as those around you. As for those who tend to be the last ones finished, I would never recommend eating more quickly, since doing so is bad for digestion. However, you should come prepared with questions to ask others so that the conversation continues to flow as you finish your food.

The Clean Plate Award: Many people were admonished as children to finish everything on their plates. As adults, this is not always a necessary, or desirable, course of action. You should moderate your food intake according to where you are, the people you are with, and how many courses will be coming to the table.

Finishing Food

Another great etiquette debate revolves around whether or not to finish all the food on your plate. There are those who say it is wasteful and insulting to your host if you don't eat everything. Others feel you must always leave a little something so that your host doesn't think you didn't get enough food to feel satisfied. I tend to leave just a little on my plate. In situations where there is an entire platter of turkey and bowls of mashed potatoes on the table, it is obvious that there is more than enough food, so you should feel free to clean your plate.

Time to Clear: When in someone's home, you may offer to help clear dishes between courses or at the end of the meal. However, if the host declines your offer, abide by this decision.

No White Lies: When you are served something that you don't enjoy, do not call attention to yourself. Find the bits that you like and eat them, and move the others around on your plate—you are not required to eat them. (Under no circumstances should you banish the unwanted food to your bread plate.) If someone draws attention to your picky behavior, simply laugh and change the topic of conversation. Do not directly answer any question about why you're not eating something. If you say that you're not hungry, but then gobble down dessert, your tablemates will know you were lying. If you go into detail as to why you aren't eating, your host may try to remedy the problem, thereby drawing more attention to you and your food instead of one another's company.

In and Out

There are differing opinions regarding the best way to remove something from your mouth that you'd rather not swallow. Some experts believe that substances should come out the same way they went in. Therefore, if you find a piece of gristle, since it went in on your fork, it should be spit onto your fork and transported to your plate. I and many other consultants find the image of this action to be disturbing. Depending on your situation, you could swallow the gristle and chase it with a swift drink of water; excuse yourself from the table and spit it out in the bathroom; or carefully extract the offending piece from your mouth with your forefinger and thumb to place on your plate hidden by your garnish. Spitting food into your napkin is a big no-no.

Stems, Bones, and Pits: If a stem or a small bone makes it into your mouth, clean it with your tongue, bring it to the front of your mouth, discreetly remove it with your forefinger and thumb, and place it on the edge of your plate. Watermelon seeds, cherry pits, and olive pits are usually spit into your closed fist.

Icky Intruders: If there's a hair or bug in your food, you'll need to size up the situation before taking any action. If calling attention to the issue is going to disrupt your big lunch interview or make your first date even more awkward, it's better to just pick around the offender. If you're at a restaurant and you decide to call your server over, whisper the problem so as not to upset your tablemates. Making the others queasy is poor form. The same philosophy applies to dining in someone's home. Announcing that there's a hair in your food at your boss's dinner party is simply not a good idea.

Bare Bones: While you may derive extreme pleasure from gnawing the meat away from a bone, this is an indulgence that is best performed alone. Unless you are at an outdoor barbecue, you should eat only those pieces of meat you are able to obtain using your fork and knife.

Quick Check: The period between the main course and dessert is an ideal time to excuse yourself if you need to use the rest room or fear you may have something caught in your teeth. Do not linger. You should return to the table as quickly as possible so others do not need to wait for you in order to begin their desserts.

78

GRACIOUS DINING

Tea Trash: When served a pot of tea, the tea bag goes into the pot. When served just a cup of tea, the tea bag goes into the cup. Once the desired flavor has been attained, you should lift the tea bag out of the cup with the aid of your spoon. Keeping the bag on the spoon, twist the string once or twice around the bag to squeeze out the liquid. Then place the spoon with the tea bag behind your cup on the saucer.

Tasteful Toasts: The best toasts are, in a word, brief. Toasts, which enhance the celebratory mood of an affair, can be given when everyone arrives at the table or just before dessert. Know that it is egotistical to drink a toast to yourself!

Fond Farewell: When the host stands signaling the end of the meal, you should stand as well. Unlike when you are excusing yourself in the middle of the meal, you should place your napkin neatly on the table (as opposed to on your chair). Then, as always, exit from the right side of your chair, and push the seat of the chair under the table as you leave.

Table Manners

Taboo Topics: The topics of conversation that are not allowed at the dinner table include issues that may lead to a contentious debate and graphic descriptions of medical ailments or anything else that might make your companions feel queasy. The goal is for everyone to feel at ease and enjoy the conversation.

Excuse Me: If you need to leave the table, for any reason, you simply need to say, "Excuse me." Do not share your need for a rest room, craving for a cigarette, or desire to make a telephone call. There is such a thing as too much information. After excusing yourself, stand up, place your napkin on the seat of your chair, push the seat of your chair underneath the table, and walk away.

No Ringy Dingies: Yes, you must excuse yourself from the table to answer your cell phone, which, of course, none of your companions heard since you switched it to vibrate before sitting down for the meal. Also note that cell phones should never be placed on the table. Doing so is considered rude as well as disgusting—after all, how often do you wash your cell phone?

Off Limits: Like cell phones, eyeglasses should never touch the top of the table. They may remain on your face, hang about your neck, or be placed in a case and stashed in your purse.

A Dab Will Do Ya: Do not blow your nose at the table. If your nose is a bit runny, you may dab it with your own tissue or handkerchief. Your napkin is not and never will be a tissue. When you need to blow your nose, you must excuse yourself from the table and proceed to the rest room. Coughing should be done into your napkin and away from the table. If you are doing a good deal of coughing and nose-blowing, there is a good chance you are too sick to be out with others. Go home.

Teeth Trouble: If you feel that there is food caught between your teeth, use the following three-step approach to dislodge it. First, close your mouth and run your tongue over your teeth to see if you can shake it free (make sure your tablemates aren't looking—they may think you're flirting). Second, take a brisk drink of water. Third, if the stubborn offender is still in place, excuse yourself from the table and proceed to the rest room, where you may remove it. In North America, it is simply not acceptable to use your knife as a mirror while you pick at your teeth. And it is certainly not acceptable to use your knife as a toothpick to clean your teeth. Should you decide to employ a toothpick in this endeavor, do so in the privacy of the rest room.

The Broccoli Debacle: One of your fellow diners smiles at you, and you cannot help but notice the enormous piece of green caught between her two front teeth. What should you do? If you catch the person's eye and quickly and silently point to your own teeth, she should pick up on the signal. If the other people at the table are caught up in conversation and you can whisper to this person without anyone noticing, you should do so. If you just cannot seem to get the point across discreetly, you may excuse yourself from the table and on your way out whisper into her ear that she has something caught in her teeth. But, people ask, what if the person is an interviewer, a big client, or a first-time date? Won't calling attention to the problem make for an awkward situation? The answer to this troubling question is that you need to evaluate the situation based on the relationship and the person involved. Keep in mind, though, that the individual will most likely discover the problem at some point and suspect that you were aware of it, but held your tongue. On occasions when I have returned home after a long day only to discover broccoli in my teeth, I wonder why no one had the courage to tell me so that I could have done something about it.

The Lipstick Debate

Yet another great etiquette debate involves the application of lipstick at the table. There are those who say that as long as you can apply the lipstick without the aid of a mirror (this does not mean you can use your knife), it is acceptable. Others, myself included, classify lipstick application as personal grooming, and as such, it should never occur in public. What's more, in mixed company, applying lipstick can be seen at best as flirtatious, and at worst as utterly inappropriate.

Handling Your Liquor

To Drink or Not to Drink: As mentioned in the restaurant section, you are not obligated to order an alcoholic beverage if others are doing so. However, you should order some type of refreshment, such as soda or sparkling water.

Follow the Leader: If you'd like to order an alcoholic drink but are uncertain whether you should, take a cue from those at your table. If the host orders an alcoholic drink, you should feel free to follow suit. If you are the first person asked, select something simple such as a soft drink. You can always change your order after hearing the selections of others by saying something like, "Oh, a glass of wine does sound nice; please change my soda order to wine." If you are hosting the meal, you have the option of speaking with your waiter in advance to instruct him as to which drinks you prefer to offer.

When in Doubt, Don't: When you are not sure if the other people at the gathering will be drinking, play it safe and order something nonalcoholic. Again, you can always change your order in the manner described above.

This vs. That: While a mixed drink, a beer, and a glass of wine all have approximately the same alcohol content, you should consider your surroundings when deciding which to order. In general, a glass of wine is a safe bet. Observe what the other people in your party are drinking and choose something similar. Please note that I did not mention shots, as these are appropriate with dinner in only the most unusual of circumstances.

Enough Is Enough: During business interactions or situations in which you are meeting people for the first time, I recommend limiting yourself to one drink, no matter how well you think you hold your liquor. Nothing dispels a positive image like slurring one's words, losing one's balance, or saying something inappropriate.

Know Your Limits

At a recent corporate function, I mentioned that few individuals improve upon their reputations (professional or social) with the increased consumption of alcohol. In response to my statement, a participant stood to announce he had already had eight glasses of wine and was feeling fine. Not only did he slur his words, he lost his balance while trying to sit down (luckily he managed to catch himself on the edge of his chair). Needless to say, my point was made clear to the rest of the group.

Dressy Drinks: Such drink garnishes as lemon and lime wedges are meant to be pushed into the drink. Clearly, paper umbrellas and fruit kabobs are a different story. If you can drink through a regular straw around the umbrella, you may do so. Otherwise, remove the umbrella and place it on your bread plate. The fruit kabobs are meant to be eaten. The thin little straws that often appear in drinks are actually stirrers and should be removed as soon as possible.

Tackling Tricky Foods

Approaching Artichokes: Steamed artichokes served with a dipping sauce are properly eaten with your fingers. Gently but firmly pull out a leaf at a time and dip before eating the tender "meat" at the base of the leaf; the rough edge of the leaf (at the top end) should be discarded on your plate. When you arrive at the center of the artichoke, remove the fuzz with your knife. Then eat the heart using your fork and knife.

French Onion Soup: This is a classic never-order-on-a-first-date dish. While fabulously tasty, French onion soup is challenging to eat because of the dense, seemingly impenetrable layer of cheese on top. Usually, you are given only a soup spoon with which to work. In order to break through the cheese, press the side of the spoon against the inside of the bowl (with the cheese wedged between the two). While there are actually special cheese knives for eating French onion soup, few establishments keep these on hand. While you may be tempted to use your dinner knife, refrain from doing so.

Long Pastas: This group includes spaghetti, linguini, fettuccine, and angel hair pasta, to name a few. It is considered barbaric to cut one's pasta. Instead, you should be provided with a large-bowled spoon to use as an anchor for your fork tines as you twirl one or two strands at a time. This is a skill that may take some time to master, so practice at home before twirling while out and about.

The World Is Your Oyster: Generally, oysters are served on the half shell and eaten with a small fork. In some more casual establishments and at the beach, oysters may be slurped (quietly) from their shells.

Slippery Snails: When served in their shells, escargots (the French word for snails) may be accompanied by a special gripper designed to let you hold the shell firmly with one hand while using a small two-pronged fork to extract the meat with the other.

How to Eat a Lobster: This tricky process requires you to use your hands, a seafood fork, a dinner fork and knife, a nutcracker, and, if you're smart, a bib.

Removing the claws: The first step in eating a lobster is to separate the claws from the rest of the body. To remove a claw, grasp the body with one hand so that the lobster remains steady on your plate and then twist the claw with your other hand.

Cracking the claws: To crack a claw, hold it close to your plate with one hand while using a nutcracker in your other to break the shell. Extract the meat with your seafood fork, using a twisting motion. Place the empty shell on the side of your plate, or discard it in the bowl brought for this purpose. (While the claws must be removed before the tail, you may eat the claw meat before or after eating the tail.)

Removing the tail: Grasp the back of the lobster with one hand and flip it over so that the belly is exposed. With your other hand, grasp the tail and twist it until it separates from the rest of the body. (The faint of heart discard the body, though some lobster lovers will extract meat from this section as well [see page 87].)

Extracting the tail meat: You may slice the tail meat out of the shell with your knife. Another method is to push the tail meat out in a swift motion through the cracked portion of the body shell. The tail meat is eaten with your dinner fork and knife. Keep an eye out for the small, black, veinlike component, which is actually the lobster's digestive tract and should be discarded.

The body cavity: As previously mentioned, some people also eat the meat from the body cavity. To break the shell, use your nutcracker; this often takes a few tries, so don't let yourself get discouraged too quickly. In addition to some meat, you'll find a couple of elements that some consider to be delicacies—namely a greenish substance, which is the tomalley, and in female lobsters, a reddish substance, which is roe. Not everyone chooses to partake of these.

The legs: Some diners so enjoy the lobster meat that they do not want any to go to waste, so they turn to the legs. These may be removed with one swift yank or a twisting motion. Sometimes, the meat is fished out of the legs using a very thin seafood fork. In more casual settings, people crack the legs with their teeth to extract the meat; this latter method is fine for lobster bakes on the beach, but otherwise you should think twice. I would not recommend eating the legs in more formal situations. In fact, at some upscale restaurants, the legs will be removed in the kitchen.

chapter five

Dating
Dynamics

Dating is often seen as a necessary evil that must be endured in order to achieve the desired result of a committed relationship. While some women look forward to dates with hope and anticipation, others are filled with uneasiness or even dread. Fortunately, as with all other social interactions, there are certain guidelines to follow that can help make the process smoother (and less painful).

Finding Mr. Right

Be Open: When you're out of school, the dating scene narrows dramatically. Be open to finding dates through a variety of sources. Ask friends and relatives if they know any single men. If you're busy, hire a professional matchmaker, sign up for an online dating service, join clubs, take an adult-education class, go to the gym, or visit your place of worship. Most of all, get out of the house. Prince Charming does not make house calls.

Cast a Wide Net: When fishing in the daring waters of the dating scene, don't be too picky too soon. Agree to meet a variety of people.

Share the Wealth: So you went on a couple of dates, but there was no love connection. Just because you didn't hit it off doesn't mean you're both destined for loneliness. Networking is not just for business anymore. Rack your brains to see if there is anyone you can introduce this person to who might be a better match. Your date should do the same for you. Hey, you never know—your bad date's second cousin might be your dreamboat.

The Next Level: In high school, it's fine to date for years and years. As an adult, however, there is a point at which the relationship must either move to the next level or end. Establish your time frame, and stick to it. If you aren't serious about a guy you've been involved with for a while, let him go so that he can find his match.

Married Matchmakers: While most married people do not miss dating, they miss the *idea* of dating and like to live vicariously through their single friends. Use this common sentiment to your advantage. Ask your married friends to set you up with suitable prospective dates—you never know....

The First Date

Start Small: Since the magic attraction factor can be elusive over the telephone, don't waste valuable time chatting for hours before you have even met. Instead, schedule a brief, low-stress, in-person first date. The best first dates with people you don't really know already usually involve a cup of coffee, an ice cream, or a drink and last for about thirty minutes to an hour. If there's more you'd like to know or share, save it for the second date.

Walk About: If you tend to be shy or have a difficult time keeping conversations going, plan a walking date. The sights you'll pass during a stroll through a historic neighborhood, a shopping district, or a farmer's market will offer countless topics for discussion.

Picture-Perfect

Some singles insist on seeing a picture of a
prospective date prior to a meeting. This is not
an advisable approach. Both looks and photo-
graphs can be deceiving. Plus, the request can
be interpreted as a demonstration of shal-
lowness—hardly an attractive trait.

Best Behavior: It should go without saying that
you need to be on your best behavior with a date.
Dress appropriately, arrive on time, and have a positive attitude. Ten minutes after the date was supposed
to begin is too late to call and cancel!

Cancellation Policy: On rare occasions, you'll
need to cancel a date because of some unavoidable
situation. As soon as you know you won't be able to
make it, call your date. If possible, reschedule while
on the phone. If you're calling at the last minute due
to an emergency, you should reschedule as soon as the
immediate crisis is over.

Keep It Light: Too many people feel a need to
review their relationship résumés in full on the first
date. While clearly you should be honest, there is no
need to use the first date as a counseling session. Allow
the conversation to remain light for the first two dates.
Find out if you even enjoy spending time with this person before sharing the intimate details of your life.

No Interviewing: Yes, finding a romantic partner
has many qualities similar to finding the right person

for a job. But do make every effort to keep the conversation for your first few interactions on a social plane. Delving into your date's full educational background, work history, and professional goals is a bit much.

Give and Take: As in other social situations, when you're on a date, the conversation should consist of a relatively even exchange. In other words, each person should have the opportunity to speak as well as listen. Monopolizing the discussion and talking only about yourself can be interpreted as self-centeredness. (For more information on carrying on a conversation, see the section beginning on page 108).

The Dollar Dance: The person who asks for the date pays for the outing. Generally, there is a bit of a dance that occurs when the check arrives; for instance, if you were asked out, your date would take the check, you would offer to pay, he would immediately refuse, and you would thank him for the lovely meal and conversation. However, things don't always go this smoothly. There are some gentlemen who will accept a woman's offer to take care of the bill. This will tell you a great deal about your companion, and you'll need to consider this piece of information before agreeing to go out again. (If you were the one asked out and truly have no intention of paying, don't offer.) How people handle money issues can be a large source of contention in a relationship, and if you're already not seeing eye to eye during the first date, this may be a sign of struggles to come. After a gentleman pays for two or three dates, it's your turn to reciprocate!

Twice Is Nice: First dates can be nerve-racking experiences, and many people are not themselves because they are so worried about making a good first impression. In general, unless the guy is absolutely horrid, you should go on at least two dates before coming to any conclusions. Stories about bad first dates often make great wedding toast material.

Be a Prude: Decide whether or not you like a guy as an individual before deciding if you want him as a romantic partner. As your grandmother might say, "A little hand-holding and cuddling can go a long way." Or as your grandfather might say, "Why buy the cow when you can get the milk for free?" I am sure you get the picture.

Saying No Nicely: After giving a gentleman two chances to click, you may find that there is simply no spark. If he asks you on yet another date, it is important to decline the request politely while allowing him to maintain his dignity. Be kind. Be firm. Be brief. "Matthew, thank you so much for the invitation to the Monster Truck Rally and Garlic Festival, but I am going to have to decline. You are a terrific guy and you have a great sense of humor, but our interests are just too different to make this work. You are going to make some lucky woman very happy. I wish you all the best."

How to Ask Someone Out

Modern Fairy Tales: Back in the olden days, a woman had to do all the household chores and then sit around crocheting doilies hoping that Prince Charming would gallop to her door on a white horse and sweep her off her feet. While many of us still fall victim to the daily drudgery, we no longer must wait passively for Price Charming to show up (which is a good thing since many men seem to have a problem with directions and will never stop to ask). In today's world, women are free to make the first move.

Three-Day Minimum: Yes, there are always exceptions, but when asking someone out, the rule of thumb is to do so at least three days in advance. So, you would need to call a man by Wednesday to ask him out for that Saturday night.

Be Prepared: Do your research prior to extending any invitation. If asking someone out for a meal, find a couple of restaurants that you think might be appropriate for the particular person. Some factors to consider are location, cuisine, atmosphere, price, and privacy. Many restaurants will fax you their menus for review. As far as atmosphere goes, save the ultraromantic and ultraexpensive spots for later in the relationship. You want to pick a place where you will both feel at ease.

Be Clear: Make sure the other person understands that you are asking him out on a date. It is best to phrase your invitation as clearly as possible. "Alex, I would like to take you to lunch on Tuesday." Or,

"Zachary, the gorilla at the zoo keeps escaping. I am dying to see him, but think it best not to go alone. Will you be my date for a trip to the zoo on Sunday?"

Be Considerate: If taking a man out for a meal, offer him a choice of restaurants, as you may not know his dietary constraints or preferences. Giving him some options will help make the date go more smoothly.

Be Sure: The day before or the morning of your get-together, call your date and, if applicable, the venue to confirm logistics.

Something to Talk About: To avoid running out of things to say, come up with a few backup topics in advance. Current events, your thoughts on the latest best-selling novel, or comments on the local sports teams are all appropriate topics to begin conversations. Starting with small talk is like warming up before exercising. Light conversation precedes meatier subjects.

Be Firm: If your date offers to pay when you invited him out, politely decline. Unless he is insistent, change the topic of conversation.

Ending a Relationship

Time and Place: Be considerate when breaking up with someone. Don't let him go right before his brother's wedding, as he's leaving for a business conference, or just after his grandmother has died. Try to pick a time when the rest of his life is on an even keel. And don't dump him in the middle of a crowded, fancy restaurant. While neutral ground is a good idea, a coffee shop is a better setting. Going for a walk is another option.

Face to Face: Unless you've been out on only a couple of dates, you should not break up over the telephone. Clearly, there are instances when this is unavoidable, as may be the case during a transcontinental relationship. But if you're living in the same area, have the decency to speak in person. Avoid putting any breakup in writing, as these letters and e-mail correspondences may come back to haunt you.

Short and Sweet: If you believe the flaws in your relationship can be worked out, by all means have a ten-hour dissection of the situation. If not, don't drag it out. Like pulling off an adhesive bandage, it's best not to prolong the process. That said, the longer you've been dating, the more of an explanation you'll need to give.

Shock and Horror: You never saw it coming. He had the audacity to break up with you. How could he? While it may be tempting to yell and throw everything that reminds you of him into the street, resist this urge and let him go. You deserve someone who recognizes what a special person you are. While it isn't easy, take the high road. Besides, you'll find that the better, cuter, nicer guys take that route, too.

This Isn't High School: While it may be tempting to tell everyone what really happened or what a jerk he is, make every attempt to avoid playing the drama queen in your own soap opera. It's an unrewarding role, and it's beneath you.

chapter six

Personal Appearance

*People-watching has long been a favorite* activity of mine. It is amazing how a person's appearance can give clues as to the type of individual she is. While some lament that in a perfect world each person would be judged by her inner being and character, I argue that our appearances are to some degree reflective of who we are. After all, our clothing does not arrive in our closets randomly. We make choices every day about where to shop, what to wear, how to style our hair, and what sort of face we present to the world. Consciously or not, most people do make assumptions based on image. You may feel that this falls into the category of "life's not fair," but you need to accept it. The trick is to acknowledge that this is how the world works and then make your image work for you.

Improving Your Image

Dress for Success: Before you leave home, think about where you are going and what you should be wearing. This doesn't mean you always need to look like you stepped off the cover of a magazine. Different outfits are appropriate for different occasions. Think of your attire as a costume for playing a part.

Better Over Than Under: It's always better to be overdressed than underdressed. Arriving in jeans when everyone is wearing a dress is far worse than the reverse situation.

Body Language: We can say so much without saying a word—it's all about body language. Are you open to meeting new people? Your shoulders should be back, your arms at your side, and your head up. Eye contact is key. In our culture, a lack of eye contact connotes a lack of confidence and possibly a shiftiness of character.

Put on a Happy Face: People often laugh when I tell them they should approach others with a smile. It seems like the most obvious advice, but judging from some of the scowls I've seen, it bears repeating. After all, would you rather speak with (or do business with) someone who is smiling or someone who is frowning? A positive attitude and upbeat demeanor can open doors.

Get out of the Gutter: Avoid using foul language in the presence of others. Cursing is not classy.

Good Grooming

A Private Affair: No one needs to know how much, or how little, effort you put into presenting your fresh face to the world. Grooming is a behind-the-scenes activity; such matters should not be taken care of in public.

Minimal Makeup: Unless you're appearing on a Broadway stage, you should wear only enough makeup to give you a bit of color. The best application makes it look like you're not wearing any cosmetics. Keep in mind that makeup does expire, in terms of what colors are appropriate (a matter driven by fashion) and the actual product itself; update your supply annually.

Professional Assistance

If you have yet to do so, consider treating yourself to a consultation with a trained image professional. This person can educate you as to what colors look best on you and how to properly apply your makeup. Some high-end makeup lines will provide the service free of charge, with the understanding that you'll purchase cosmetics from them. Independent image consultants charge for their advice, but don't expect you to purchase anything. Ask friends and family members whether they can recommend someone. This type of session can be an eye-opening and confidence-building experience.

Fresh Face: Makeup application should take place in front of a mirror, at home, before you face the world. Your fellow commuters should not be subjected to your cover-up mission as you attempt to conceal your zits. This applies to all commuters, whether traveling by train, plane, or automobile (there is nothing as annoying—not to mention dangerous—as being stuck behind someone who is using the rearview mirror to apply eyeliner instead of paying attention to the road).

First Aid for the Face: If your skin needs extra help, don't ignore it. Visit a dermatologist so that your skin gets the care it needs and any problems can be treated.

Fresh Breath: Anyone who has ever worked with someone who needs a mint knows how important fresh breath is to those around you. Whether it is a spray, hard candy, breath mint, or dissolvable strip, be sure to carry something in your purse that you can easily pop into your mouth.

Neat Nails: Eyes may be the windows to the soul, but hands are the gatekeepers. While weekly professional manicures may not be within your budget, basic maintenance is required. Hands should be clean (this includes the area underneath your nails), and nails should all be the same length. If your nails are polished, the color should be appropriate for your line of work and enhance your image rather than stealing the show. Once your polish begins to chip, remove it immediately.

Best Foot Forward: If you're going to be bold enough to wear sandals or other open-toe shoes in public, make sure your feet can stand up to the attention. They should be clean, with the dried skin removed from your heels. Your toenails, too, should be clean, as well as shaped and, if possible, polished. When you go out with disgusting feet, people cringe and wonder what other skeletons you may be keeping in your closet.

Nail No-No's: Do not clip your nails in public. Like other aspects of personal grooming, this should be taken care of in private. Not only is nail cutting an extremely unattractive procedure to observe, but it also causes nail clippings to scatter everywhere—ick. You should also refrain from biting your nails—doing so indicates a sense of nervousness and childishness; plus, chewed-on nails are not a pretty sight.

No Excavating: Whether it involves your ears or your nose, please make sure that all digging is a solitary pursuit. No spectators allowed.

Scents Sense: Personal hygiene is a given. Showers and/or baths taken at regular intervals are essential.

Beyond that, you should be aware of your personal scent. Take into consideration your perfume, shampoo, conditioner, hair products, soaps, lotions, and even laundry detergents; all of these combine to form your personal fragrance. As many of those with whom you come into contact may have allergies, you should keep any scent light—it should not be overpowering. Unless the person you are speaking with is in hugging range, he should not be able to smell you. Less is more.

No Spraying: Perfume should never be applied in a public space. In addition to falling into the realm of personal grooming—thus making it a solo activity—putting on perfume has the added element of possibly triggering an allergy attack in someone nearby. Be considerate and leave the perfume bottle at home.

Hair Hints: If your hairstyle at your twentieth high-school reunion is the same as in your senior class photo, it's time to visit the salon. Many personal appearance decisions are affected by modern trends. Know the difference between passing fads and true style. While you don't need to match the Parisian runways, you should have a hairstyle that fits in with the current decade. Find a hairstylist you trust and really listen when this professional says it's time for something new.

Horrid Habits: Imagine watching your favorite news anchor chewing gum, twirling her hair, cracking her knuckles, swinging her legs, or squirming in her seat. These actions are more in line with the behavior of a child than an adult. When adults fidget nervously, they make those around them uncomfortable. Do your best to remain calm and poised.

Attire Advice

Suiting Up: If you got a call to interview for your dream job tomorrow, would you have an appropriate outfit for the occasion? You should have a dark skirt suit and a matching shirt in your closet, ready to wear at a moment's notice (you should also have matching pumps and skin-colored panty hose on hand). This all-purpose suit can take you far. It's appropriate for not only interviews, but also presentations and most religious services (including funerals). And it can provide building blocks for other outfits. The skirt could be paired with a sweater twin set for casual days at work; the jacket could be paired with new jeans to dress up an "around town" outfit.

The Little Black Dress: Appropriate for cocktail parties, semiformal events, and special evenings out, the little black dress is a versatile classic and, hence, a wise investment. Many can be dressed up or down with the help of accessories.

Comfort Wear: Even when you are simply running errands, it is important to look presentable. If you were to run into an old friend (or your biggest client) at the grocery store, you should not find yourself feeling mortified by your appearance. It is possible to be comfortable and look respectable.

Gym Wear: If you work out regularly, treat yourself to an outfit appropriate for the activity. Cutoff jeans and free T-shirts should be saved for gardening in the backyard. And don't forget to give yourself the necessary support—for both your chest and your feet.

Never Wear: Garments that you should never wear out of the house include anything ripped, stained, or missing buttons; anything that is too tight; anything that went out of style a decade ago; and anything that you would put on to work in the garden or clean out the garage.

Firm Foundations: People often give little thought to what goes under their clothing. But clothing fits better when worn with the proper undergarments, which can help smooth curves and contain bulges. While the right bra and panties may not transform you into an instant supermodel, they will work wonders for your wardrobe.

Out of Sight: The name truly says it all; undergarments should be worn under your clothing—and they should be hidden from view. Unless you work in the world of adult entertainment, the lace pattern of your underwear, your bra straps, your panty lines, and your slip should not be showing.

Accessories Make the Outfit: While there are many different views regarding accessories, I advocate selecting ones that will show your attention to detail and provide a glimpse into your personality. Some classics to have on hand include black pumps with a matching purse, pearls (necklace and earrings), and a larger bag (generally in leather) that can serve as a briefcase for work or a carry-on when traveling. When donning accessories, pick ones that coordinate with your outfit—just as you would select a shirt to coordinate with your skirt when getting dressed.

chapter seven

Meeting and Greeting

Sometimes it seems as though certain people were born with the gift of gab. They are perfectly at ease chatting up others, and they never seem to be at a loss for something to say. But the truth of the matter is that being a good conversationalist is actually a learned skill. This means that with a bit of coaching and practice, anyone can mingle like a pro. So what are the basics for meeting and greeting? Read on.

Carrying on
a Conversation

Know Yourself: Always be prepared to give a self-introduction. Your name gets you only halfway there. You also need to include a little something about yourself—it is this shared tidbit that will propel the conversation, cuing the other person to ask you a question. "Hi, I am Lauren Fleisher, sister of the bride." "Nice to meet you; I am Stacy Kamer from Boston." "Hello, I am Alesia Latson; I teach confidence."

Introducing Others: The basic rule is that men are introduced to women, younger people are introduced to older people, and lower-ranking individuals are introduced to higher-ranking individuals. When making an introduction, include each person's full name and then mention something that they may have in common in order to help get the conversation started. For instance, "Miss Pennyworth, may I introduce Mr. Jonathan Worthier. Jonathan, this is Elizabeth Pennyworth; she has just returned from safari." Or, "Grandmother, this is my roommate Ellen Samberg. Ellen, this is my grandmother Ms. Estelle Halpern. Grandmother, Ellen has just published her first poem."

Pleased to Meet You: When you are introduced to someone or introducing yourself, it is appropriate to shake hands (for information on how to do this properly, see page 114).

Be Prepared: Before going to any event, have a few backup topics of conversation on hand so that you have something to say if there's a lull. There are many typical subjects, including current events, movies, concerts, books, school/work, hobbies, family, travel, sports, and pets. Choose the ones that interest you. When in doubt, you can always talk about the weather!

Party Trick

Before going to a cocktail party or a similar gathering involving mingling, have a little something to eat. This way, you can focus on the conversation without being distracted by the desire for food. It is challenging to be witty when you are starving. And shoveling food into your mouth is no way to meet new people.

Play Catch: Think of conversation as a game of catch. You catch the ball, hold it for a few seconds, then throw it back to the other person, who catches it, holds it for a few seconds, then throws it back to you. Repeat. Good conversations involve give and take. If you find that you are not talking at all or that you are doing all of the talking, something is off.

Keep the Game Going: Just as it affects the image you project, body language can go a long way toward keeping a conversation going. Your body should face the other person, shoulders squared to hers; your stance should be open, rather than closed off (in other words, don't cross your arms or hide your hands in your pockets). Last but not least, maintain eye contact. All of these actions indicate to the other person that you are receptive and interested in what she has to say.

All Ears: Make sure that the other person knows that you're listening. The message can be conveyed by nodding your head or by voicing an occasional "um-hum."

Continuous Conversation: Another way to keep the conversation flowing involves the way you phrase things. Ask open-ended questions—ones that require at least a sentence as an answer. "How do you know the host?" "What makes you say that?" "What was your favorite vacation?" "Tell me about...."

The Receiving End: When asked a question, avoid giving a monosyllabic answer. Even if the person asks a "yes or no" question, expand upon your response with some sort of explanation to keep the conversation rolling. Do not put the other person in the position of having to do all the work by giving her one-word answers. If the conversation seems boring to you, change the subject to one that interests you more.

Practice Makes Perfect: Like any other skill, conversing should be practiced. Whether it is the cashier at the local bagel store or the town librarian, try carrying on a brief conversation about the weather or current events. (That said, don't strike up conversations with strangers when you're alone, at nighttime, or in any potentially dangerous situation!) The more you practice, the more comfortable you will feel, and the better you will be at small talk.

Smile: As mentioned with regard to general appearance, smiling is important. Good conversationalists are also good at smiling. Wouldn't you rather speak to someone who is smiling than someone who's not?

Timing Is Everything: Most cocktail party conversations (in other words, discussions that take place in social situations where everyone is standing up and mingling) should last, on average, about five to eight minutes. This is a chance for you to meet new people, not close a business deal or set a wedding date.

Cocktail Coordination

Cocktail party situations are ideal for people who are left-handed. I like to say that at cocktail-style events, everyone is a lefty. You should carry your food or your drink in your left hand so that your right is free to shake hands and exchange business cards.

Information Exchange: If you've enjoyed speaking with someone, ask for her business card or telephone number so you can get in touch at a later date. Once the other person has handed you her card, offer yours. However, you should never offer your card first. Carry your business cards with you wherever you go—you never know when someone will ask for one.

Safety First: If someone asks you for your number and you do not feel comfortable giving it out, don't. Manners matter, but safety first. And don't fill someone with false hope by giving a fake telephone number. Rather, find a phrase that works for you—perhaps, "I am flattered you would ask, but my life is terribly busy right now!"

Graceful Exits: While often considered one of the most awkward aspects of social etiquette, once learned, extricating oneself from a conversation is a remarkably simple task. As the conversation begins to lag, look the person in the eye, extend your right hand for a handshake, and say, "It was a pleasure to meet you." You could also use "I enjoyed speaking with you" or "It was great to catch up." Any pleasantry that indicates the conversation is over will do.

Excuses to Eschew: When trying to remove yourself from a conversation, don't tell the other person that you're going to the bar, as she may very well decide to join you. Also, never say you need to use the facilities. First of all, this is more information than a new acquaintance needs to know. Second, the other individual may decide to join you. Third, do you really want your encounter to end on a note that involves your bladder?

Maintain Control: Being the one to bring a conversation to a close gives you control as to how it ends. This is especially important if you don't want to share contact information. Extricate yourself before the discussion gets to that point.

Buddy System: If you're attending an event with a friend, work the room alone. After all, if the two of you wanted to sit in a corner together and talk, you could have done that at home. Mingling on your own will not only force you to talk to others, but will also encourage others to talk to you—it is often too intimidating for individuals to break into a conversation that is already in progress. Do check in with your buddy periodically, though. You may even want to consider having some signals or key words to indicate when you're ready to leave.

Shyness and Social Situations

A large part of life involves speaking with other people. If you are truly very shy, you should enroll in an adult-education course or volunteer at your favorite charity. The more you put yourself in talking situations, the more practice you will have and the better you will feel. Sometimes part of confidence is faking it until we feel it. You could also enroll with one of the many organizations that offer training in public speaking and interacting with others.

Handshakes

First Contact: One of the most basic social skills is a good handshake. While few people will admit to giving a bad handshake, almost everyone has been on the receiving end of one at some point.

Hand Check: Before entering a situation where it is likely you'll be shaking hands, make sure your hands aren't icy or clammy. If you tend to have cold fingers, wear gloves outside and make every attempt to warm your hands before shaking. When you arrive at a function, you can dash into the rest room and run your hands under the hand-dryer or warm water. If your hands tend to be on the moist side, see your doctor to make sure that nothing is medically wrong, then experiment with different lotions to find one that will help reduce the amount of perspiration in your palm; lastly, keep a 100 percent–cotton handkerchief in your pocket to blot your hands before shaking.

Web to Web: The "web" between your index finger and thumb should hit the web of the other person.

Finger Curl: Your fingers should then curl around the bottom of the other person's hand.

Proper Pressure: You should apply enough pressure to the other person's hand so that this individual can feel that you are there, but not so much as to make his knees buckle.

Shake, Shake: Shake the other person's hand up and down two or three times before releasing. This movement should be a small and comfortable one—not too vigorous.

Beginning and End: For those occasions when you shake hands, you should shake at the beginning of the interaction and again at the end.

Then and Now

In the olden days, a man would not extend his hand to a woman unless she extended hers first. Nowadays we are gender neutral, but it's all about rank and age. The highest-ranking or older person should extend her hand first. (This does not always happen, and occasionally the lower-ranking person will be penalized for not shaking the boss's hand.)

Taboo Topics

Background Basics: It is best not to comment on someone's race (or even ask where the person is from) unless the individual has raised the topic. Even asking about someone's accent can be iffy, since the question may be perceived as a racial one.

Individual Identity: A person's religion or cultural heritage can be a highly charged topic. Again, unless the individual has brought up the subject, avoid this area. There are those who try to push their own point of view in the hopes of persuading a person to change her religion or cultural identification. In the vast majority of situations, it is simply unacceptable to proselytize to a new acquaintance.

Bandages and Braces: As tempted as you may be, do not ask what any bandages or devices that provide physical assistance are for, as this is really none of your business. If the individual cares to discuss his medical history with you, he will bring it up.

And Baby Makes Three: While asking a married couple when they plan to have children may seem like the most natural question in the world, unless you are a very close friend, this is a no-no.

Big-Ticket Items: When someone tells you she has just purchased a house or tickets for a fabulous vacation, if your natural reaction is to play "The Price Is Right," bite your tongue. It is not acceptable to ask.

chapter eight

Everyday and Every-So-Often Encounters

When we are in situations that we aren't familiar with, we sometimes run the risk of offending an individual without meaning any harm. We may have the best of intentions, but our lack of experience causes us to do or say the wrong thing. Some of us, for instance, may not have had much contact with people who are ill, pregnant, or physically challenged. But by becoming educated in the proper manners, we can demonstrate respect in such interactions.

Etiquette of Illness

Make an Offer: Instead of saying "Call if you need anything" to a caregiver or a person who is ill, offer to perform some specific service. The former approach places a burden on someone who already has plenty on her mind to figure out what it is that you can do to help; it also puts this person in the often uncomfortable position of having to ask. Those in need will be much more likely to take you up on an offer if it is for a specific action.

The Three Cs—Cooking, Cleaning, Caring: If you aren't sure what you can do to help, here are some tasks that you might offer to perform for someone who is ill.

✦ Bring meals (include warming instructions), but beware of dietary restrictions.
✦ Clean the house (or pitch in to hire a service).
✦ Walk the dog.
✦ Do a load of laundry.
✦ Pick up dry cleaning.
✦ Carpool the kids.
✦ Provide transportation to the doctor's office (be sure to arrive early so that there is no chance of missing the appointment).
✦ Shop for groceries.
✦ Fill the car with gas (or move the car so it won't be towed).

Visit, Visit, Visit: Days can be long for a person who is sick, so visits are often welcome. Be sure to call before stopping by, and keep your visit short so as not to exhaust the individual. Here are some helpful hints.

◆ Wash your hands as soon as you arrive (whether at someone's home or the hospital) so as to reduce the possibility of spreading germs.

◆ Bring magazines or books.

◆ Be ready with topics of conversation (the patient has probably not been doing much and, hence, may have little to say).

◆ Keep the conversation light and upbeat.

◆ Listen, listen, listen.

◆ Bring board games to provide entertainment and distraction.

◆ Take the patient out, if her health permits.

Always Ask: Yes, you should ask, "How are you?" in a sympathetic tone. Then take your cues from the patient's response as to whether further discussion about the condition is wanted. Some patients actually find it easier to share how they are feeling with people outside their immediate circle, as they don't want to worry their close friends and family.

Sharing Sob Stories: Part of human nature is to form connections by sharing like experiences. However, when someone is ill, you should refrain from this practice. Being sick is a highly individualized experience. Do not presume to know how the other person feels.

Call in the Troops: When someone is ill, having a caring community can make all the difference. Recruit others to visit, bring meals, and pitch in however possible.

Keep in Touch: Once the crisis has passed, friends and family will often say, "We were thinking of you." But those affected by the illness need to know you care while they are going through it. Whether you choose to mail a card, send a gift basket, or call, make a special effort to stay in touch.

Pregnancy Parameters

Don't Ask: Her ankles look swollen, she has been a bit green in the morning, and she has not worn anything tailored in weeks…. No matter what "signs" you think you see, do not ask a woman if she is pregnant. If she isn't, she will be insulted. And if she is expecting, she may not be ready to share the news with you. Hold your tongue, and wait for an announcement.

Don't Tell: Once a woman has publicly announced her pregnancy, resist the urge to tell your favorite horror story. Talking about miscarriages, stillbirths, and weeklong labors is not appropriate. Pregnant women are well aware of these occurrences and do not need to be reminded of them.

Hands Off: Those round bellies are terribly tempting, almost magnetic, but you may not touch a pregnant woman's tummy unless you have been invited to do so.

Suddenly Superstitious: Many people become superstitious during pregnancy. Don't be insulted if expectant couples demonstrate reluctance to discuss the baby or answer certain questions evasively—and don't push them on the subject. Because of superstitious beliefs, many couples will not share the baby's name or gender, and some prefer not to have a baby shower until after the child is born.

Giving Gifts: Because of superstition, some couples may not want gifts until after the baby is born. Unless you are attending a baby shower, refrain from giving a present until after the birth. If something does go wrong, coming home to a nursery full of toys and baby clothes can be difficult to bear.

Raining Pink and Blue

Baby showers are often held when a couple is expecting their first child, and these events tend to be hosted by close friends. (While it is acceptable to have a shower for a second child, the gathering is a much smaller affair, if it is held at all.) Nowadays, those who are expecting often register for gifts. You may purchase an item from the registry or select something on your own. If you are a mother, you might give an item that you could not have lived without. If you don't spend much time around babies, you might pamper the mother with a gift certificate for a pregnancy massage or a pedicure. I like to give first-time mothers the movie *Parenthood*. It gives them a small taste (with a dollop of humor) of what to expect!

Acknowledge Loss: Occasionally, a pregnancy comes to a premature end. This is obviously a difficult time for the couple, and every individual reacts differently. Some people want to be alone, while others want to be comforted. Some return to their routines quickly, and others don't. Reach out, but follow the individual's cues regarding whether you should give more outward support or provide some space.

Baby's Arrival

Call First: Before you visit a new family at the hospital, call to see if visitors are welcome (and don't be offended if they're not). Different people react differently to the birth experience. Some new parents want lots of friends and family to stop by as soon as possible. Others prefer to have private family bonding time.

Prime Form: Do not even think about visiting the new family unless you are in perfect health, as you don't want to risk spreading infection. Anyone with even a sniffle should stay home.

Go with Gifts: If you are able to visit, don't go empty-handed. You may have a special present that you are planning to give later (or you might have given something special already at the shower), but you should arrive with a little token—perhaps "real" food for the parents (undoubtedly a welcome change from hospital sustenance), a rattle or stuffed animal for the baby, or balloons for the room. (Note that latex balloons are not allowed in most hospitals. Mylar is preferred for safety reasons.)

Hospital Visits: Giving birth to a child is an exhausting experience. Watch the new parents for cues as to when you should take your leave. A short visit (fifteen to twenty minutes) can take a lot out of a brand-new mom.

Flowers in Lieu: If you are unable to visit, sending a flower arrangement is a nice touch. Even the more comfortable hospital rooms tend to be rather institutional, and flowers help to liven up the surroundings. Many hospitals have in-house florists that you can order from if you aren't familiar with any local providers.

Manners and the New Parents

Birth Announcements: As is the case with a wedding announcement, if you receive a birth announcement, you are not required to send a present. However, it is a gracious gesture to congratulate the parents by sending a card.

Baby Talk: A new child is all-consuming, so almost all discussions with a new parent will revolve around the infant. Feel free to ask the child's name, why that name was chosen, and if the parents are getting any rest. You might also ask to see pictures of the baby or give hints (if you have any to share) on helping the baby sleep through the night.

Don't Touch: New baby skin, new baby smell—these are irresistible to many, but you cannot simply act on your impulse. Watch the new parents for cues. Some people are more protective than others. You may ask to hold the baby, but if the answer is no, just wait. Within a few months, the parents will undoubtedly be happy to hand off the child to anyone who offers.

Be a Baby-Sitter: One of the best gifts that you can give new parents is the gift of time. If you are comfortable doing so, offer to watch the baby for a while so that the grown-ups can run errands, take a nap, or even go out on a "date." If baby-sitting is not your thing, you might try to help by bringing over dinner, going grocery shopping, or pitching in with the housework.

Beware of the Breast: New mothers do what new mothers do—feed their babies. In our culture, breasts have been socialized to be sexual, when their true function is to nourish the young. If the mother needs to breast-feed, ask if she prefers you to step away. Otherwise, avert your eyes until the baby has latched. Most women are able to feed their babies without others even noticing.

Assisting People with Physical Challenges

Offer First: When interacting with someone who you think might need your help, offer your assistance and wait for the individual to accept. Do not touch anyone before your offer has been accepted.

Blindness: To offer assistance to a blind person, you should verbally address him as you approach and ask to help. Most blind people who do accept will expect you to move to their right and offer your left elbow so that they can follow your lead. Do not grab a person's arm and push him along.

Deafness: When speaking to someone who is deaf, be sure to look directly at her. If the individual has a hearing aid or reads lips, this position will make it easier for her to understand you.

Wheelchair Use: Often the best assistance you can provide for a person in a wheelchair is clearing a path that will permit navigation. When speaking to someone in a wheelchair, you should try to find a seat for yourself so that the individual is not forced to endure a conversation looking up at you.

Mind Your Manners: When meeting a person who is physically challenged, no matter how curious you are, do not ask about the disability. If he wants to share this information with you, he will do so on his own. And for goodness' sake, don't stare.

chapter nine

Here
to
There

As you know, etiquette provides the
framework for interactions between people. These
interactions don't occur only while we are at home,
at work, and at such venues as restaurants and theaters, but also while we are in transit to and from
these places. It is just as important to demonstrate
manners while in motion as when you are in more
established social situations.

Traditional Doors

Open Sesame: When approaching a closed door—whether it leads to a residence or a private office—you must knock (or ring the doorbell) and then wait to be invited inside.

Allow Me: When approaching a door along with another person, the younger, lower-ranking, or more able-bodied person should endeavor to open the door for the older, higher-ranking, or less able-bodied person.

Hold On: Be sure to hold the door for anyone who may be behind you (and do take a quick glance over your shoulder to avoid accidentally letting the door close in someone's face).

Inside Out: When people heading in opposite directions arrive at a doorway, those who are already inside the building or room must be allowed to exit before those who are on their way in may enter.

Revolving Rules

Who's First? When a revolving door is already in motion, the older, higher-ranking, or less able-bodied person should enter first. When this type of door is not already moving, the younger, lower-ranking, or more able-bodied person should enter first to set the door in motion.

Keep Moving: When exiting on the other side, don't stop directly in front of the revolving door, as those behind you will have nowhere to go. If you are unsure as to which direction your destination is, step aside to figure it out so you don't cause a pileup.

Pull Your Weight: Unless you are physically unable to do so, once you've entered a revolving door, you are responsible for doing your share of the pushing—there are no free rides. That said, this is not an amusement park ride; be considerate of others, and don't send the door whipping around.

Elevator Etiquette

Right of Way: Let those trying to exit an elevator do so before you attempt to step into it. Following this simple rule will make the process easier for everyone involved.

Take Control: If you're the person closest to the control panel, offer to press buttons for other passengers.

Hold It: If you see another person coming, hold the elevator. How would you feel if the situation were reversed and no one held the elevator for you?

No Holdups: If you run to catch the elevator and find other passengers inside, yet the rest of your group is trailing behind you, it is best to let the elevator go and wait for the next one. You don't want to inconvenience others.

Patience Is a Virtue: The elevator does not move any faster just because you keep pressing the button. The only effect that this action may have is to irritate those around you.

To Speak or Not to Speak: If you're carrying on a conversation in an elevator, beware of what you say. Don't say anything that can't be repeated—even if you don't know the other passengers. Also do not subject your fellow riders—who can't escape until they reach their floors—to any discussion they might find unpleasant (no one wants to hear about your gastrointestinal problems). Last but not least, keep your voice down—in such tight quarters there's no reason to shout.

Have a Nice Day: Small talk with other passengers can be pleasant, but it isn't a requirement.

Easy Exits: If you are standing at the front of a crowded elevator, when the doors open at a floor, step out to allow others to exit. If you are in the middle or at the back of an elevator and must get by others to exit, say "Excuse me." Pushing and shoving are not allowed.

Escalators

Stand Aside: Years ago, as a small-town girl living in London and riding the Tube, I learned very quickly that there are lanes on escalators: "standers" on the right, passers on the left. (The English may drive on the opposite side of the road, but their escalator lanes are the same as ours.)

She Who Hesitates: Proceed swiftly and smoothly when stepping onto or off an escalator. If you suddenly change speeds, the people behind you have no option but to bump into you. When stepping off, if you are confused as to which direction you need to head, move out of the way before stopping to figure it out.

Get a Treadmill: As tempting as it may be to run up the down escalator or run down the up escalator, please refrain from doing so. Not only do you run the risk of injuring others, but those teeth at the edge of the escalator steps can be dangerous. There are better ways to get some exercise.

Navigating Sidewalks

Who Walks Where? When you are strolling on a sidewalk with a date, your date should position himself between you and moving traffic. When you are with children, you should position yourself between the children and moving traffic. Safety first.

Walk with a Purpose: Walk with your head up, shoulders back, and eyes taking in your surroundings. Keep your arms swinging gently or resting at your side. (Don't look like a victim.)

Traveling in a Pack: When walking down the street in a group, make sure that others can get around you. Don't monopolize the sidewalk.

Don't Block Traffic: If for any reason you decide to stop on the sidewalk (perhaps to chat with a friend or figure out where you're going), step out of the way so that you don't hinder others.

Walk and Talk: For some inexplicable reason, some pedestrians can't seem to talk on a cell phone and walk in a straight line; instead, they wander from side to side as though they've had a little too much to drink. If you're going to talk on your cell phone while walking on the sidewalk, do not let it interfere with your forward progress. Be aware of those around you. (Also note that if you decide to make a call from the street, there is bound to be a lot of background noise, which the person on the other end might find disturbing.)

Airplanes

High Style: I love the pictures of travelers during the early days of airplanes. They always look as though they're headed to a party. Nowadays, people look (and sometimes smell) as though they've come directly from the gym. Considering the cramped quarters of most airplanes, do your best to ensure that your attire will not offend your fellow passengers. (Keep in mind, too, that even if you're traveling to or from a warm climate, the temperature on airplanes is usually cool, so dressing in layers is your best bet for comfort.)

Size Matters: While it would be nice if there were unlimited space for luggage in the passenger cabin, this is simply not the case. Bring on board only what you are positive will fit in the overhead storage compartment or underneath the seat. Do not bring a huge bag and expect your fellow passengers to heave it overhead for you.

Food for Thought: If you're bringing your own sustenance onto the plane, avoid foods with odors that other passengers might find offensive, such as tuna. Being confronted with an unpleasant smell can make the trip unbearable for those around you.

Crossing the Line: When seated, do not let your limbs, personal belongings, or blanket spill over to another person's seat. Most likely, the person sitting next to you spent a good deal of money—or forked over a lot of frequent flyer miles—for her seat, and she is entitled to every millimeter of it!

The Friendly Skies: Your movements should not disturb others. Avoid fidgeting, and be careful not to step on anyone's toes when getting in and out of your seat (by all means, politely ask your neighbor to stand so that you don't have to climb over him). Remember, usually there are not only people next to you, but in front and back of you as well. Refrain from kicking the seat in front of you, and be gentle when putting your seat back or folding up your tray.

Keep It to Yourself: When using headphones (whether watching a movie or listening to music), keep the volume down so as not to bother those around you. Your neighbors should not be able to hear the sound coming from your listening device.

Stop the Stampede: At the end of a flight, passengers often begin gathering their belongings and jockeying for exit positions before the plane has come to a complete stop. Unless you're late for a connection, wait your turn.

Trains and Subways

No Snatching Seats: While some passenger trains have assigned seating, most—especially commuter rails and subways—don't. Passengers who have been waiting the longest should board first, the exception being those who may need extra assistance.

Subway Civility: Allow those passengers exiting the train to do so before you get on. This tactic facilitates the process for everyone involved.

Give It Up: If an older or less able-bodied person needs a seat, you should always offer yours.

Saved Seats: When you were in elementary school, it may have been fine to save a spot on the bus for your friend, but when commuting, you are not allowed to have your belongings take up a seat as if you had reserved it for your imaginary buddy. This goes double for putting your feet or wet umbrella on the seat.

Cancel That Call: Prolonged cell phone use in a situation where others are trapped and forced to listen to you is not good behavior. Ideally, you should not speak on a cell phone while you're on a train. If you must communicate some critical information that can't wait, such as your arrival time, keep the conversation brief and your voice low. If the connection is so bad that you need to yell, hang up and call the person back later.

Stinky Situations: When trapped with strangers in a small space, you should do all you can to avoid offending fellow passengers. This includes bathing on a regular basis and using deodorant (which, of course, you should be doing anyway), keeping your shoes on, and not eating food with offensive odors. If you do eat or drink, pick up after yourself.

Courtesy Is Contagious

Years ago, when I lived in the city and rode the subway regularly during rush hour, I performed a bit of an experiment. When I saw someone who needed a seat more than I did, in a firm voice (so that others could hear) I would offer mine. Interestingly enough, on the days that I did this, others would follow suit at subsequent stops. However, on those days when I was standing and had no seat to offer, rarely would others give up their seats to those in need. Remember that your good example can set off a positive chain reaction.

Automobiles

Diligent Driver: As the driver, you must assume host responsibilities in the car. Be sure to get rid of any rubbish in advance so that the vehicle is tidy; know how to get where you're going or be willing to ask directions; and be prepared to play music that is acceptable to most of your passengers. Last but certainly not least, and this should go without saying, you must pay attention to the road and obey the laws for safe roadway travel.

The Perfect Passenger: As a passenger, you must avoid distracting the driver. And if you are a frequent passenger who isn't a member of the immediate family, you should offer money for gas or occasionally take the driver out to dinner.

Sit and Spin: When wearing a dress for an evening out, a woman should be helped into the car by the driver or her date. To breeze through the process gracefully, hold the other person's hand to steady your body as you delicately seat yourself sideways in the car (in other words, your bottom should be on the car seat and your feet on the ground). Once securely in this position, place your hands on the seat and rotate your legs into the car so that you are facing forward. To exit the car, reverse this procedure.

The Door, Madame: When you're chauffeured by a professional driver or out for a romantic evening, it is nice to have the car door opened for you. However, if you're out with friends or in a hurry, as long as you are physically capable of doing so, there is no reason you shouldn't open the door yourself.

Keep Your Cool: Clearly, road rage falls into the category of unacceptable behavior. We all know that driving in traffic can be frustrating; however, swearing, swerving, blocking, racing, and making finger gestures is not only unproductive, but hazardous. Practice deep breathing, or leave yourself extra travel time.

Tips on Tipping

Tipping is an important part of our culture.
The amount of a gratuity is based not only on the quality of service you receive, but also on your budget and the region in which you live. (If you're finding that your budget is really stretched when you hit the end-of-year tipping season, or you are always counting out change to cover the tip, you may be living a little above your means.) The following guidelines for gratuity amounts are general; consult local resources for numbers that are specifically appropriate for the area in which you live.

Out and About

Restaurants

Maître d': $10 for a special table, complicated reservation, or large party

Coat check: $1 per item

Wait person: 15 to 20 percent of the total bill (the busing staff receives a cut from this)

Sommelier: 8 to 15 percent of the wine bill

Bartender: $1 per drink when at the bar

Rest room attendant: $1—even if she doesn't hand you a towel (she is there to keep everything tidy)

Buffet/counter service: 10 percent of the bill

Personal Care

Hairstylist: 15 percent of cost for services

Colorist: 15 percent of cost for services

Shampoo person: $1 to $5, depending on how much she's done (some give scalp massages and mini facials!)

Etiquette Evolution

It used to be that if your hair was cut by the salon owner, you didn't tip. Nowadays, this isn't always the case, as some owners don't add the tip into the cost of the cut. Ask at the front desk about the tipping policy.

Facialist/waxing technician: 10 percent

Manicurist: 10 to 15 percent

Pedicurist: 15 to 20 percent

Masseuse: approximately $10 an hour

Physical therapist: no tip, but do give an end-of-year gift

Child Care

Baby-sitter: tip when the kids have been especially taxing or if you arrive home later than expected

Day care: no tip, but do give an end-of-year gift

Movers and Shakers

Movers: $10 to $50 per mover, depending on the size of the move, the number of steps, and the number of heavy pieces

Lawn/snow crew: no tip until the end of the year (see page 145)

Cleaning person: if you've just had a big party or if you've requested special services, $10 an hour above and beyond what you agreed to pay, with a $20 minimum

Grocery bagger: $1 per bag if this person has brought the bags to your car (done only in certain locales)

Licensed repair person: no tip

Building superintendent: $3 to $20, depending on the issue and time of day

Delivery people: $1 to $3 for flowers, balloons, pizza, and other food deliveries; employees of large shipping companies are not tipped

Newspaper deliverer: 50¢ to $1 a week, or $20 to $50 at the end of the year (how good is his aim?)

Dog walker: $10 if he also takes in the mail or waters plants for a week, or whatever you deem appropriate if he helps with a pet emergency

Taxi driver: 10 to 15 percent, provided you weren't taken on an unrequested tour of the city

Limousine driver: 15 to 20 percent, unless the tip is already included (be sure to check)

Travel Tipping

Bellhop: $1 to $2 per bag

Maid: $1 to $2 per person per night (left on a pillow on the bed so that it's clear the money is for the maid)

Room delivery: $1 to $2

Room service: 15 to 20 percent, unless already included (be sure to check)

Valet: $2 to $3 when the car is picked up, or $1 to $2 at the time of drop-off and at pickup

Doorman: no tip to open the door or guide you to a taxi waiting at a stand; $1 to $2 to flag down a cab for you

Concierge: $5 to $10 for a special service such as acquiring tickets to a sold-out show, obtaining last-minute dinner reservations for a local hot spot, or researching where you can take your poodle to have her nails painted pink

Tour guide: $1 to $2 per person per day

End of the Year

The end of the year is your chance to show your appreciation for those who make your life easier. How much to give is a highly subjective matter. Amounts depend upon your relationship with the person, local norms, and your financial capacity. Bills should be new and crisp, and placed in an envelope with a card or a note of appreciation. When appropriate, a small gift can be given along with a monetary tip. Here are some general guidelines.

Child Care

Baby-sitter: two nights' pay

Nanny: one week's salary for each year of service or, after the first year, 10 percent of yearly salary

Au pair: one week's salary for each year of service or, after the first year, 10 percent of yearly salary

Apartment Living

Custodian: $20 to $30

Doorman: $25 to $100

Handyman: $25 to $50

Superintendent: $25 to $100

Parking attendant: $20 to $30

Home Care

Cleaning person: one week's salary

Dog walker: one day's pay

Garbage person: $20

Regular delivery person (newspaper, dry cleaning, groceries, etc.): $5 to $20

Lawn/snow crew: $10 per person, a bit more for the boss

Personal Care

The following are applicable if you're a regular customer.

Hairstylist: cost of one session

Colorist: cost of one session

Shampoo person: $5 to $20

Facialist/waxing technician: cost of one session

Manicurist/pedicurist: cost of one session

Masseuse: cost of one session

Gifts Instead of Gratuities

The following individuals do not receive end-of-year tips; however, a small gift accompanied by a note of appreciation is appropriate.

Mail carrier

Teachers

Licensed repair people, such as plumbers and electricians

Physical therapist

Day care provider

chapter eleven

Keep
in
Touch

When we talk about social interaction, we often think about face-to-face situations. However, much of our communication doesn't involve in-person encounters. We call, we send e-mail, some of us even still write letters. As with any other type of interaction, these exchanges are more likely to go smoothly if certain established guidelines are followed.

Incoming Calls

Third Time's the Charm: You should pick up the phone when you hear the third ring. If you answer too soon, you'll likely startle the caller; too late and the caller is bound to become impatient.

Selective Screening: Unless you're a receptionist or answering the phone is an integral part of your job description, you are not obligated to answer the phone. That's right. The fact that the phone is ringing doesn't mean you need to drop everything to pick it up. If you have an answering machine or voice mail, it may even be more time-efficient to screen calls and return them later than to answer on the first go-around.

Say It with a Smile: When you do choose to answer the phone, be sure to sound as if you actually want to talk to the person on the other end. Believe it or not, if there's a smile on your face, the person on the other end can hear it in your voice. So smile!

Message Material: Beside every telephone, there should be a pad of paper and at least one writing implement. Having these essentials in place allows you to jot down notes or take messages without compelling the person on the other end to wait while you dig around. You should also set up a workable system within your household to ensure that everyone actually receives messages once they've been taken.

May I Take a Message? If you've answered the phone and the person with whom the caller wishes to speak is not available, you should offer to take a message. Be sure to obtain and pass on the person's full name and telephone number. If the caller has a specific message to be relayed, write that down, too.

Banished to Voice Mail: Your voice mail or answering machine should not be a black hole. Check your messages regularly, and respond promptly. Ideally, you should try to return social calls within twenty-four hours, but if you're particularly busy, calling back within seventy-two hours is acceptable, as long as an immediate response is not necessary. Business calls should be returned within twenty-four hours.

Tireless Telemarketers

While being polite is a virtue, you don't need to extend every courtesy to telemarketers. Most are instructed never to hang up and will keep you on the line as long as possible in the hopes of parting you from your hard-earned money. Ask to be taken off the master call list.

Outgoing Message: There are a few points to keep in mind for the outgoing message on your voice mail or answering machine.

Be brief: Callers should not be compelled to listen to an outgoing message that lasts more than thirty seconds.

Identify: At a minimum, state your number so that callers know they've reached the correct machine. While some people include their names on the outgoing message, if you live alone, you may not want to do so for safety reasons (some single women will even use the pronoun "we" instead of "I" on the message).

Remind: Despite years of leaving messages on machines, people often forget to leave their name and/or number, so be sure to prompt them.

Waiting Game: When call waiting first appeared on the scene, I was a huge fan. To not have callers receive a busy signal was wonderful. Now I am glad technology has moved on so that calls can be routed directly to voice mail. Call waiting should be answered only when you are expecting an important call and have forewarned the first caller. Otherwise, you should allow the second call to ring into voice mail. If you don't have voice mail, get it or get rid of call waiting. In the meantime, if you absolutely must pick up, be brief and tell the second caller you'll phone her back. Unless it's an emergency, you should not hang up on the person you were originally talking to in favor of the second call.

Outgoing Calls

Telephone Timing: Keep your friends' lifestyles in mind before placing a call. Those with kids may be up at the crack of dawn, while those without kids may be up until the crack of dawn. If you have any doubt as to whether it's a safe time to call someone, wait until you're sure.

Who Goes There? Perhaps you've had a conversation similar to the following:

> "Hello?"
> "May I speak with Ms. Magnotta?"
> "May I ask who is calling?"
> "Are you Ms. Magnotta?"

As the caller, it is your responsibility to identify yourself before the person on the other end divulges any information.

Guessing Game: While you may think that your voice is as distinctive as Fran Drescher's, when placing a call, you should always identify yourself. Whether the cause is a poor connection or a poor memory, it's no fun trying to figure out who is calling after an individual has already launched into a conversation—or when retrieving a message.

Remember to Repeat: Always give your name and number twice when leaving a message so that the recipient does not need to play the recording more than once. Be sure also to speak slowly and clearly.

It is also helpful to mention the purpose of your call (this needs to be said only once).

Multitasking and the Telephone: Remember, the phone picks up your voice as well as many other sounds in the area. This means you should be very careful about chewing, typing, and, well, flushing while on the phone. If the person on the other end feels that you're not devoting all of your attention to her, she might feel insulted—and rightly so.

For information specific to telephone etiquette in the business world, see page 168.

Common Courtesy and the Cell Phone

What Civilized People Know: When the ringing of your cell phone might disturb others, turn off the phone or set it to vibrate.

Backup Plan: If there is the potential for you to receive an emergency call, let others know where you are going and provide an alternative for contacting you. For instance, if a loved one is very ill and you are headed to a restaurant or the theater, leave the phone number of the establishment on your cell phone's outgoing message so that you may be reached in case of emergency.

Do Not Disturb: If you are at the theater, in a restaurant, at a wedding or funeral, or in any other situation where others are trying to pay attention or are unable to move away from you easily, you should not answer your phone (and, of course, the ringer should be turned off). If you think you might receive an emergency call and your phone vibrates in any of the above situations, you must remove yourself from the presence of others to speak (this may mean going outside, to a vestibule, or to the ladies' lounge).

Insulting Interruptions: If you are with other people—at a social gathering, on a date, or on an interview—your attention should be focused on them. It is rude to answer your phone in such a situation.

Drivers Beware: If you are in your car, please pull over (where safe to do so) before using your phone. Studies have shown that the act of talking on the phone (not just dialing or holding the phone) contributes to driver error.

For Your Ears Only: Be aware that if you're talking on your cell phone while out in public, your discussion can be overheard. If the topic of your conversation is not an item that can be printed on the front page of the newspaper, postpone the discussion until you have some privacy.

Where to Wear? I have been told by the fashion aficionados that clipping your cell phone to your belt is "so 1990s!" Keep these communication devices out of sight—in a pocket, purse, or bag.

E-mail Etiquette

Be Brief: E-mail is intended for short informational messages. Keep in mind that with some e-mail programs, it is possible for the recipient to read just the first three lines of a message without ever opening it. So make those first few lines count!

Be Pleasant: Watch not only what you say, but how you say it. A message with a heated tone is known as a "flaming" e-mail. Using all capital letters is considered YELLING. If there's a word or sentence you want to stress, use an asterisk on either side of it to *emphasize* it.

Punctuate Properly: If you are going to take the time to send an e-mail, take the time to do it right. Use proper punctuation, upper- and lowercase letters, and correct spellings (run spell check before sending). This little bit of extra attention is a demonstration of respect to the recipient since it makes your e-mail easier to read.

Be Selective: Think carefully about who really needs to see the information you are sending. "Reply All" and "cc" can be useful features, but they're not necessary in all circumstances.

Be Careful: If you have e-mail at work or are sending a message to someone at his workplace, think twice about the content. E-mail is considered the property of the employer and may be monitored. Some companies may even specifically prohibit the use of e-mail for personal matters.

Be Timely: While e-mail is an instantaneous way of transmitting a piece of correspondence, unless otherwise stated in the message, an immediate reply is not required. One week is the standard period within which you should respond to a social e-mail. However, in the business world, a one- or two-day turnaround is required.

Better Beware: Before forwarding that e-mail that promises free merchandise or warns against some horrid happenstance, be sure it is accurate. There are thousands of blatantly untrue myths circulating in cyberspace.

For information specific to e-mail etiquette in the business world, see page 170.

Letter Writing

Paper Products: Ideally, letters should be written on stationery or note cards. There is something to be said for the formal, luxurious feeling of high cotton-fiber content in watermarked paper, while handmade sheets containing pressed flowers offer a touch of elegance for more casual situations. For informal correspondence, a whimsical card can bring a smile to the face of both the sender and the recipient.

Personalize It: No matter what your social standing, it is a good idea to acquire personalized stationery, which can bear your full name, your first name, or your monogram. The envelope may be left blank or bear your address on the back flap. Personalized paper can be ordered from stationery stores, copy centers, or individual dealers. You should consider ordering both note cards (folded or not) and writing sheets. Keep in mind that the higher the percentage of cotton fiber, the nicer the paper. When it comes to printing techniques, engraved stationery is the most formal (and expensive), but thermography offers a similar look at a lower cost.

Typing vs. Writing: If you are composing a lengthy letter or have horrid penmanship, typing may be the logical choice. However, short notes, thank-you notes, condolence notes, and love letters really should be handwritten. Handwriting is more personal and has a warmer effect.

Proper Pen: Letters should be written in pen. Pencil has a tendency to smudge and fade. The more formal the note, the darker the ink color should be.

Why Write?

There are few simple pleasures as gratifying as opening your mailbox to discover a hand-written note from a friend. In our fast-paced world, the idea of sitting down and composing a note by hand may seem incomprehensible. But consider this: when the great-grandmother of my friend Jesse died, the family members spent hours sitting, talking, and reading the letters this beloved woman had saved over the years. Computer files just don't have the same effect.

Take Your Time: A well-written letter is never rushed. Think about where the recipient is, what she is doing, and what the two of you have in common. You may even wish to compose the letter on scrap paper first to avoid making mistakes on your good stationery. If you are a few lines into a long letter, or are proofreading a note, and spot a mistake, you may cross out the error and write your correction neatly above it or in the margin. While this would be unacceptable in business, there is a bit more leeway in social correspondence.

Spelling Made Simple: When writing a letter, all words must be properly spelled. The dictionary is your friend. Use it.

Grammar: Take care to use proper grammar when writing a letter. If you have trouble in this area and are sending an important piece of correspondence, you might ask someone with a better feel for grammar to read a draft. Sometimes, just reading the letter out loud will help you to catch any mistakes.

Staying Connected

It is interesting to note that people who are successful, both socially and professionally, devote a good deal of their energy to keeping in touch. They do not call just because they want something. They call to catch up or share some information they think the other person might find interesting or useful. They write birthday cards, anniversary wishes, and thank-you notes. They send interesting articles that made them think of the other person. They pass along names of people, books, and restaurants. They understand that building friendships, networks, and support structures takes time and effort. Keeping in touch and maintaining relationships is a lifelong success skill—and anyone can do it.

Sign-Offs and Signatures: Like all good things, all good letters must come to an end. The way in which you bring your piece of correspondence to a close will depend upon the nature of the letter and your relationship with the recipient. Typical sign-offs include "Sincerely," "Best regards," "Warm regards," "Yours truly," "Hugs and kisses," and "Love." Of these, "Sincerely" is the most formal. And, of course, don't forget to sign your name.

Condolence Notes

Every Second Counts: You should handwrite a condolence note as soon as you learn of a death. The longer you put it off, the harder it will become. If you end up putting it off for a bit, you should still send a note. It is important for the mourners to know that you care.

Content: What exactly you write will vary depending on your relationship with the deceased as well as your relationship with the person to whom you are writing. Keep the focus of the note on the deceased and your thoughts of the living. If you knew the deceased, you might want to share one of your treasured memories of this person.

Dear Mrs. Morlino,

I was saddened to learn of your husband's passing. Whenever we bumped into each other around town, he would have a kind word and smile. Seeing him always brightened my day. And my daughter adored the way he would shake her hand silly while pretending she was shaking his too hard. He will be missed.

Sincerely,
Lizzie Jacobs

Dear Cousin Ann,

As you know, I never met Mark's mother. From the stories you recounted, I could tell that she was a remarkable woman. I was especially impressed with her ability to teach both Mark and your children table manners through games and jokes. You and your family are in my thoughts and prayers.

Love,
Sarah

Be Kind: Everyone copes with loss in a different way. Telling a mourner how he should feel, how lucky he is, or that the death was "for the best" truly does not help him feel any better.

Thank-You Notes

When to Write: If someone took the time to give you a gift, you should take the time to write that person a note expressing your gratitude. You should also write a thank-you note when someone has made an extra effort on your behalf, such as referring a client to you, hosting a meal, or getting you an interview for a job. And whenever you have an interview, you should send a thank-you note to the interviewer. All thank-you notes should be sent as soon as possible.

The Personal Touch: Thank-you notes should be handwritten—in ink, of course. This has a warmer effect than typing.

Better Late Than Never

It is never too late to write a personal thank-you note. Yes, you should write the note as soon as possible—within a few days of a gift-giving holiday and within a week of a birthday party, for example. But even if you have gone beyond the proper time frame, you still need to send a note. Be sure to apologize for your tardiness, but don't give excuses. The later the note is sent, the longer it will need to be (so do it when you're supposed to)!

What to Say: Sincerity is the most important aspect in writing a thank-you note. Mention the gift or action specifically, and let the recipient know why you appreciated it. Here are some examples.

Dear Ryan,

It was so nice of you to remember my birthday! Thank you so much for the beautiful writing paper. As you know, I am an avid correspondent. I look forward to using the stationery and will think of you each time I do.

> *Yours truly,*
> *Katharine*

Dear Rebecca,

Lunch was fantastic! Thank you so much for taking me out for a fancy meal. The food was delicious and the company superb. I look forward to reciprocating in the near future.

> *Best regards,*
> *Judy*

chapter twelve

Life
at
Work

Navigating the political scene at work is never easy. Because some rules and practices vary depending on the industry or individual company, you'll need to take your cues from those around you and modify your actions accordingly. However, there are some standards with regard to conduct that you should know and follow. The more professional and polished your behavior, the better off you'll be.

Secrets of Success

Capable Clothing: Like it or not, people do make judgments about ability based on appearance. You should make the best impression possible by always looking polished and professional. This holds true even if your office is business casual.

Know the Code: Before you start any new job, ask about the dress code. Your first clue should have been what the people who interviewed you were wearing at the time. Many companies have highly detailed, written dress codes. Appropriate office attire varies depending on the industry, the geographic region, the individual company, and even the specific departments that exist within a company. Typically, finance is a conservative field, whereas fashion and entertainment are more casual and trendy. Your ability to determine what is appropriate for your position will contribute to your success at the company.

Wear a Watch: Keeping your eye on the time is important. You should arrive for meetings, and work in general, a few minutes before you are due.

Late Arrival: When you do find yourself late for an appointment, call ahead to let the other party know that you're on your way. When you arrive, enter as discreetly as possible. When appropriate, apologize, but do not rationalize or offer excuses. Keep the focus of the discussion on business—you don't want to waste any more of the other party's time.

Be Equipped: When heading to a meeting, be sure to bring any necessary background paperwork, paper and writing implements for taking notes, and business cards (you don't need the latter if the only people at the meeting are your coworkers). You want to inspire confidence in those around you—not appear to be ill-prepared or disorganized.

Keep Your Cool: While a colleague might make you want to scream, don't. Take some time to cool off, gather your composure, and reassess the situation. Organizations have long memories for poor behavior.

Be Diplomatic: Undoubtedly, you and your coworkers will have differences of opinion regarding how a certain matter should be handled. Assuming you are in a position to speak up, you need to convey your point diplomatically. In other words, you need to be able to disagree without being disagreeable. The way in which you express your disagreement will have a powerful effect on how your point of view is received.

Courtesy to All: Treat all fellow employees with respect, regardless of where they rank in the company hierarchy. Present a professional face to everyone.

Be Your Boss's P.R. Person: Regardless of your feelings toward your boss, it is important to make her look good to other members of the team and to clients. Part of your job is to make sure that your boss is informed of important matters and is never caught by surprise.

Set Expectations: Whether working with fellow employees or clients, it is important to realistically estimate the scope and time frame for your portion of any project. Give yourself extra time for delays and emergencies to arise. Whenever possible, complete your portion ahead of schedule so that others know they can rely on you.

Networking vs. Idle Chatter: While being known as the office gossip is not good for your career, hiding in your cubicle is also a mistake. It is important for you to be aware of what is happening in your workplace. You should know who the important players are and be sure they know you. Get up from your desk, make plans with colleagues for lunch, and volunteer for cross-functional projects.

Get Involved

Participating in company-sponsored activities can be a great way to meet or get better acquainted with others who work for your organization. Sign up to help plan the company picnic, join one of the company sports teams, or offer to help coordinate the philanthropic drive.

Selective Listening: When you work in an open office environment, selective listening is a must. As tempting as it may be to eavesdrop on your coworkers, you need to be able to tune out other people so that you can get your own job done. If you absolutely can't help but overhear, under no circumstances should you interject yourself into the conversation or give advice on the matter later.

Keep It Down: When on the phone or having a discussion with others—whether personal or professional—don't be excessively loud; undoubtedly there are others around you who need to be able to concentrate on what they're doing. If having a radio on is permitted in your workplace, keep the volume low.

Your Mother Doesn't Work Here: At the office, it is necessary to pick up after yourself. From throwing away the bag that your lunch came in to picking up your coffee cup when you leave a meeting, you need to tidy up after yourself. If there's an office kitchen, don't leave your dirty dishes lying around on the counter or in the sink. And if you spill something, wipe it up!

Refrigerator Rights: It should go without saying, but don't help yourself to food in a common fridge that doesn't belong to you. You also shouldn't leave your own food in the fridge for too long—others should not be subjected to the stench of your spoiled leftovers.

You Are the Company: Anytime you make contact with people outside the office, you become a representative of the company. Whether communicating in person, on the phone, or via written correspondence, you should be as polished as possible. Avoid slang, misspellings, and remarks that may be a bit too casual for a business interaction.

Professionalism and the Phone

Always Update: If you leave a dated or special outgoing message on your voice mail, update it as needed. If you will be away or unable to check your voice mail for more than seventy-two hours, be sure to mention that on your outgoing message. When possible, you should also provide an alternate contact.

Test Drive: After you've recorded a new outgoing greeting, listen to it to make sure that it sounds the way it should and that the information is accurate.

Pass It On: Calls should never be passed along to another person without a proper introduction. First, you must tell the caller the name and number of the person you're going to transfer him to, just in case the connection doesn't go through. Then, before you actually forward the call, you must tell the person who will be receiving the transferred call who the caller is and why he is calling.

Speakerphone Strategies: Speakerphone is a useful tool, but it needs to be used with caution. You must always inform the person on the other end that you're putting her on speakerphone, as well as let her know who else is listening to the conversation. Whether you're having a discussion or simply checking voice mail, speakerphone should be used only in a room with a closed door.

Exit Stage Right: It never fails—there is an inverse relationship between the chattiness of one party and the workload of another. While ringing your own doorbell may work at home to exit a conversation, this option is usually not available at work (unless you work at home). Luckily, there are a number of "verbal doorbells" that are just as effective. Here are a few lines to help close a conversation: "Thank you for your time—I don't want to keep you." "I know you must be busy—thank you so much for calling." "I would love to speak about this some more, but the work is just piling up on my desk." All of these closings, spoken with the proper tone and tact, can ease the discussion to an end.

Cradle with Care: When you hang up the phone, take care to do so gently. Slamming the receiver down will not be appreciated by the person on the other end if she still has the phone to her ear. And make sure that the call has really been disconnected before you say anything to others; if the receiver didn't quite make it into place, the person on the other end might overhear your conversation.

For additional information regarding telephone etiquette, see page 148.

Business E-mail

Be Specific: The subject line is your friend. Write brief, descriptive titles. This will not only alert the recipient to the matter at hand before opening, but also enable him to find the message easily if there is a need to refer back to it.

The Girl Who Cried Wolf: Prioritize your e-mail appropriately. If you send everything high-priority, the little red exclamation point will begin to lose its meaning.

Be Yourself: Don't assume that the recipient will know who you are or be familiar with your organization. You may need to give your title, company, and phone number.

Be Professional: Do not hide behind your computer. E-mail should not be used to avoid phone conversations or face-to-face interactions.

Be Compliant: In the office, e-mail is a professional tool. The messages in your mailbox should be work-related. Many companies reserve the right to monitor your workplace e-mail.

Be Polite: As more and more of our daily work occurs over the Internet, more of us will experience professional relationships that exist only over the Web. Strive to make every interaction a pleasant one.

For additional information regarding e-mail etiquette, see page 154.

Gracious Good-byes

I Quit! While it is tempting to include a manifesto of the company's ills in your resignation letter, you are better served by keeping such thoughts to yourself and making the content as simple as possible. A resignation letter needs only three elements: the date of your last day working for the company, your contact information (address and phone number), and your signature.

Plan Your Timing: Once you have decided to leave a company, you often become a lame duck. Plan your announcement and your final departure time carefully. Be sure to factor in time for a replacement to be found and some training to take place, but do not linger. Most companies have a standard resignation time frame. Read your company manual carefully before submitting your resignation. Also, be aware of the company culture. Some organizations have a stated two-week notice for resignations, but will escort you to the door the day you submit your letter.

Farewell Festivities: In some instances, your boss might throw you a going-away party. However, you are not allowed to plan your own. Your exit could be more political than you think, and your former coworkers will need to ally themselves with the organization. If you have a few close friends at work, you might arrange to meet them for dinner, but don't announce your plans to the entire group.

Exit Interviews: Many companies interview outgoing employees to gather information. Answer all questions judiciously. Some exit interviews are confidential, while others are not. In addition, you don't want to burn any bridges. Boomerang employees (ones who leave a company only to be hired back a few years later) are becoming more and more common.

It's a Small World: If you specialize in a certain field, it is highly probable that you and the people you are leaving behind will cross paths down the road. Keep relationships positive and communication open. You never know when you might see (or need) your former boss or coworkers.

Take the High Road: Not only is it less crowded, but you're less likely to be in a position of regretting something you said or did. Leaving a company can be a stressful and unnerving time, but you need to keep your wits about you. Don't yell at anyone, don't destroy company property, don't take office supplies, and don't disparage the organization to clients, the media, or others in the field. Doing so will only reflect negatively on you.

conclusion

Clients often cringe when I tell them I love to read antique etiquette books for fun. But these instructional guides—which offer snapshots of the time in which they were written—have the power to transport me to a different era. Discussing such matters as how to send a well-written Mailgram and how a gentleman should tip his hat when meeting a lady on the street, these books from yesteryear open a window to another world. Yet, as I travel back in time via the yellowing pages of these tomes, I realize that the more things change, the more they stay the same. While we no longer leave calling cards at people's homes or send letters of introduction with friends moving to new cities, the underlying principles remain constant. Etiquette is about respecting yourself and showing respect toward others. It is about having confidence in yourself and making those around you feel comfortable. No matter what the era, if you know what behaviors are appropriate in any given situation, you are able to relax and enjoy yourself. When you relax, you put others at ease. And, when you put others at ease, they enjoy being with you.

Etiquette is fascinating because it involves so many different areas: history, sociology, psychology, gender issues, race relations, and technology. It is my hope that this book has not only helped you to conduct yourself in a more polished way, but also sparked some curiosity and interest in you regarding human behavior.

index